"*Internships for Today's World* offers something for any educator or business contemplating real-life work experiences for students. The book provides solid rationales for incorporating internships into schooling, examples of validations and feedback from students, business leaders, and educators, as well as details that could only be provided by authors who spent time in corporate management and more than a decade providing 'matches' among students and intern sites at the nation's premier and longest-standing external learning school, City-as-School, New York City. What to look for in prospective sites, how to make matches, pitfalls to avoid, linking assessment to practice—all are covered. The book can offer much to the field and to individuals at any stage of creating and maintaining quality external learning experiences." —**Steve Phillips**, former superintendent, Alternative High Schools and Programs, NYC Board of Education

"McLachlan and Hess have written a book that offers real hope for providing meaningful learning experiences for students that complement and fortify in-school learning. A recent national study demonstrated that only 28% of students are intellectually engaged in our schools, but internships offer opportunities for 100 % engagement. Realistically, school is not an ideal environment for providing all the necessary opportunities for becoming an adult. Instead, school is a particular kind of environment, honoring individualism and cognitive development. It imposes dependence on, and withholds responsibility from, students. We have lost sight of young people's potential for responsibility. Internships, as outlined in *Internships for Today's World: A Practical Guide for High Schools and Community Colleges*, provides opportunities for accepting responsibility and offering real opportunities for students to feel and to be useful. It offers a practical guide for establishing a quality, sustainable internship program. This book provides conclusive evidence of the power of internships for student engagement and learning." —**Jerry Diakiw**, faculty of education, York University, former superintendent of schools York Region District School Board, Ontario

"What better way to prepare our young people for the future than to give them authentic access to real world experiences? As a 30-year high school principal, I will view my most fulfilling legacy as having established internships for ALL students in my schools. To this day, former students describe these dynamic opportunities as among the most powerful in their educational careers. This book provides a road map for secondary schools and community colleges to build internships that are authentic, engaging, and result in our young people making highly personal and informed career decisions." —**Jay Lewis**, retired high school principal, associate dean, school of education, Hofstra University

"Internships are one of the most powerful transformative experiences that a high school or community college student can have. They literally become a reality-based journey that opens the student's mind to the world beyond the school's walls. They are unquestionably a superior preparation for college and careers. *Internships for Today's World* is a must-read for high school and community college educators. It offers a practical guide to developing meaningful internship programs. The authors' in-depth insights and recommendations equip all educators with the tools to bring a high quality internship program to their schools." —**Matthew M. Mandery**, EdD, director Nassau County Senior Year Network; executive director Nassau County Principals Association

"The authors bring the world of student internships, externships, practicums and projects into an exciting and yet utilitarian book that will aid the imaginative educator in creating "real world" experiences for learners." —**Robin Calitri**, former principal, Southside High School, Rockville Center, New York, principal of the year, NYS

"Joan McLachlan has understood and practiced learner-centered, experiential education for decades. I first met her when she was doing that at City-as-School, one of the oldest and best public alternatives. She has co-authored a book about the core of that program—internships. In using this book the reader will understand what internships are and how to help students do them effectively. As we continue in the new millennium this approach will greatly increase in significance, as more and more new jobs are created that didn't exist just a few years ago." —**Jerry Mintz**, director, Alternative Education Resource Organization (AERO)

"*Internships for Today's World* by Joan E. McLachlan and Patricia Hess is that rare occurrence—a practical handbook and blueprint for setting-up internships as well as the philosophical rationale for doing so. Field-tested practices and implementation guidelines developed through research and best practices are yours to research, to assess, and to apply to your individual learning community—be it high school, university, or organization in the private or public sector. This book—a thoughtful, pragmatic offering—underscores the need for true development of a work-based partnership which serves the intern as a career exploration experience and the learning resource (the organization offering the internship), a rationale for the internship, most welcome staff assistance, and possible staff recruitment. This book will provide a welcome resource, saving hours of false starts, conceptual cul-de-sacs, and conserve energy used to design, to create, and to implement effective internships." —**Richard G. Safran**, co-founder (and former principal) of City-As-School High School, NYC

"*Internships for Today's World* is a superb primer on the whys and hows of an effective internship program. Its clear language and comprehensive scope will enable any school to set up such a program and extract maximum benefit for its students. I cannot praise the book highly enough." —**Joan Chabrowe**, former City-As-School resource coordinator

Internships
for Today's World

Internships for Today's World

A Practical Guide for High Schools and Community Colleges

Joan E. McLachlan and Patricia F. Hess

ROWMAN & LITTLEFIELD
Lanham • Boulder • New York • Toronto • Plymouth, UK

Published by Rowman & Littlefield
4501 Forbes Boulevard, Suite 200, Lanham, Maryland 20706
www.rowman.com

10 Thornbury Road, Plymouth PL6 7PP, United Kingdom

Copyright © 2014 by Joan E. McLachlan and Patricia F. Hess

British Library Cataloguing in Publication Information Available

Library of Congress Cataloging-in-Publication Data

McLachlan, Joan E., 1943–
  Internships for today's world : a practical guide for high schools and community colleges / Joan E. McLachlan and Patricia F. Hess.
      pages cm
  Includes bibliographical references and index.
  ISBN 978-1-4758-0601-4 (cloth : alk. paper) — ISBN 978-1-4758-0602-1 (pbk. : alk. paper) — ISBN 978-1-4758-0603-8 (electronic)
  1. Internship programs—United States. I. Hess, Patricia F., 1943– II. Title.
  LC1072.I58M35 2014
  331.25'922—dc23   2013046606

∞™ The paper used in this publication meets the minimum requirements of American National Standard for Information Sciences—Permanence of Paper for Printed Library Materials, ANSI/NISO Z39.48-1992.

Printed in the United States of America

To Frederick J. Koury, who believed in real-world learning.

Contents

Preface		ix
Acknowledgments		xv
Introduction		xvii
1	Key Elements of a Quality Internship Program: *Getting It Right from the Start*	1
2	Internship Site Development: *Internships Don't Just Happen*	17
3	Placing Students in Internships: *One Size Does Not Fit All*	31
4	Monitoring Students in Internships: *Providing a Guiding Hand*	45
5	Supporting Sponsors in Internships: *Building a Strong Partnership*	51
6	Seminars for Reflective Learning: *Making Sense of It All*	59
7	Evaluating Internship Learning: *Putting It All Together*	69
8	The Predictable Stages of Internships: *No Surprises*	85
9	The Power of Internships: *Real Schools, Real Stories*	97
Afterword		105
Appendix		107
Glossary		121
Works Consulted		125
Index		129
About the Authors		135

Preface

Look ahead thirty years. Can you predict the changes that will occur to our educational system? Can you predict the challenges schools will be facing? Do you know what the state of our economy will be? Can you predict the jobs that will be needed to help our economy continue to grow? Now look back thirty years. Were you able to foresee the challenges facing education today? Were you able to predict the roller coaster economy? Could you have predicted the impact technology and globalization have had on the economy and education? Could anyone have predicted the hold social media would have on our young people?

Over these past thirty years change has been tumultuous. And we believe that change will continue to be rapid. We have learned from our years of experience in education and business that we need to help our young people meet the challenges that change presents. We need to give them opportunities to build the skills they need for the twenty-first century. And we need to help them to adapt to further changes in their lives by ensuring that those skills are transferrable. We need to ensure that our young people have the skills they need to navigate their way in a new economy.

We know that internships help students develop twenty-first-century skills. Our experience has, again and again, shown us that students learn valuable skills in an internship. We now see more and more comprehensive high schools, academies, charter schools, AP programs, senior projects, CTE and tech programs, and community colleges partnering with businesses and organizations so that their students have the opportunity to build new knowledge and skills in the real world. We continue to see excited and engaged students talk about their internships and their learning. We continue to hear students say that their internship experience has helped them shape their career. And we hear over and over from internship sponsors about their enthusiasm and willingness to work with our young people.

We believe that internships are for every student. All students, whether they are in high school or at a community college, deserve the opportunity to gain an understanding of the world of work, learn skills that can be transferred between jobs and industries, apply their school knowledge in the real world, test out a career to see if it is right for them, and build their self-belief so that they can achieve success in this changing world of work.

But today's young people also present a challenge to educators and employers. While they are proficient in technological skills, they spend long hours on social media with their friends, they want instant feedback, and, at times, want someone else to take responsibility for their career. They are often not ready to step into the world of work whether directly from high school or college. Our experience has taught us that internships give young people a chance to build relationships with adults and colleagues in the workplace and learn valuable life skills. These relationships can help ease our young people away from a total focus on social media to real and meaningful face-to-face exchanges with colleagues and adults in the real world. And this is an important step for any young person as he or she moves forward into adulthood.

While we don't have a roadmap for the next thirty years, we know that change will continually be with us. What we can do is ensure that our young people are ready to move into the workplace and meet the challenges presented to them.

PURPOSE: WHY WE WROTE THIS BOOK

We have written this book because our experience has taught us that internships have the power to engage all students. They give opportunities for all young people to develop the skills they will need as they prepare for the next stage of their life.

We have worked with schools to set up programs and enhance their current programs. We know the challenges faced by schools from constant testing to having only limited resources. But we know that even with these challenges a quality internship program can be established and sustained.

We know that every school can develop a quality internship experience for students that suits both the needs of the student and the school. Schools may find that internships work best when linked to their specific curricula, or are part of their senior projects, or challenge the notion of the "senior slump" or are closely linked to organizations in their community. We know that a quality internship program can be tailored to a school's specific needs.

This book starts with the premise that internships are critical in building the skills needed for today's economy and that many of those skills will help our young people deal with changes they will face in their lives. It sets out, in detail, all the elements needed to start, build, and sustain a quality internship program. And it gives specific detail on how to build those twenty-first-century skills that will benefit all our students.

WHAT MAKES THIS BOOK UNIQUE?

This book is written from over twenty-five years of experience in education and business. Unlike books that give personal experiences and chronicle stories of successful interns or books that give a general overview of the benefits of internships, we look in detail at all the elements that are necessary for a quality internship program in the twenty-first century, from start-up to building a sustainable program. It is not a "wish list" for an internship program but detailed field-tested practices and implementation guidelines developed through research and best practice. We use our many years of experience setting up and implementing internship programs in a variety of different schools from urban high schools, community colleges, alternative schools to small rural schools to define, in concrete terms, all the elements that make an internship program successful. And we bring those elements into the twenty-first century. We use our experience in working with a variety of for-profit and non-profit organizations in defining the skills and behaviors required for success, especially for entry-level jobs. We are very specific about how these behaviors are defined, not by educators but by organizations, and we look at how internships can help develop these behaviors in our young people before they enter the workforce.

Internships are experiential learning and we know that in order to be of value any internship needs to have a solid curriculum to help shape the student's experience. We offer specific suggestions on how to build an effective, field-tested curriculum that maximizes student learning.

Schools want to know how to ensure that their interns are staying on track. We give specific guidelines on how to find the most appropriate internship for students and how to monitor the interns when they are at their work site.

Schools want to know that any experiential learning can be assessed. We offer specific suggestions on how to evaluate this learning giving field-tested examples of evaluation techniques and assessment rubrics.

We strongly believe in the value of internships for our high school and community college students. And we believe that for any internship to have maximum value it needs to be structured, have student input, focus on building twenty-first-century skills, and have robust evaluation.

We have set forward those elements of an internship program that we know through research and practice make for a successful experience for the intern, the school, and for the sponsoring organization. And our many years of experience in education and in business have also enabled us to look at internships in the context of a changing economy. While internships need to be driven by the school, we have balanced academic learning with the practical skills required by today's organizations.

HOW TO USE THIS BOOK

This book is a resource for those who are concerned that our young people need to develop the skills that will help them succeed when they leave school and enter the workforce or continue in further education. It is for all those who believe that an internship is not just a feel-good experience for the student but a vehicle whereby the students can learn and build important skills that will carry them forward in their career and in life. The book can be used in its entirety for those who want a complete picture about setting up and sustaining a quality internship program. Or individual chapters can be used to add to an already existing program. Checklists and sidebars can be referred to for additional ideas or as a program audit. We have also included templates and examples of forms and rubrics that we have used for schools to adapt and tailor to their own specific needs.

The *Introduction* sets the context for internships in today's economy and looks at the challenges in starting and sustaining a quality internship program. We then focus on those Key Elements that will make a program a success in *Chapter 1*. *Chapter 2* brings the Individual Learning Plan into the twenty-first century in defining goals and activities that will build skills of problem solving, critical thinking, and creativity along with solid academic skills. Finding internship sites and placing students is the focus of *Chapter 3*. In *Chapter 4* we highlight what needs to be done to monitor students in their internship placement. *Chapter 5* looks at the role of the sponsor and ways of helping the sponsor ensure that the intern has a positive learning experience. *Chapter 6* identifies some of the skills employers want and how these skills are built through reflective learning. Here we also look at the role of the Mentor as coach in the workplace setting. Authentic Evaluation is the focus of *Chapter 7* and suggestions of how to evaluate the students' learning are given. In *Chapter 8* we highlight the challenges some interns present as they move through their placement. And *Chapter 9* looks at successful internship programs in a variety of settings. The *Appendix* contains examples of forms and learning plans.

AUDIENCES

Our audiences are high schools, community colleges, and state and local policy makers who want to develop or enhance learning opportunities for students in the real world. High school principals, community college presidents, and administrators will find that the book gives a comprehensive overview of a quality internship program. The detailed chapters will ensure that nothing is lost or overlooked when designing a program. The introduction makes the case for internships in the twenty-first century and chapter 1 sets out the key elements of a quality internship program so that administrators know how internships can fit into their schools' strategy and mission. Additional chapters highlight the role of the teacher/internship coordinator in implementing a program.

Teachers or educators who are designing an internship experience for a small class or for a large group can use *Chapter 1* as a checklist for their program. They will find the details in *Chapters 2–7* to be invaluable as they develop and implement their program. *Chapter 8* gives clear insight to the stages experienced by an intern, and most importantly sets forth what a teacher might expect from interns as they move through their placements. *Chapter 9* illustrates how schools have met the challenges of setting up an internship program tailored to their specific needs. All the chapters define the role of teacher/coordinator in creating successful learning. Checklists will ensure that all elements get included in any new program.

Teachers and program coordinators who are already implementing an internship program can use *Chapter 1* as a checklist for their program. They can also use individual chapters for additional ideas and activities that will ensure that students are developing the skills they will need in the real world.

State departments of education, local school boards, and others who are concerned about transitioning young people into the workforce and into further education will find a strong case for internships. The book can be used as a resource guide as they work with schools and other organizations in building opportunities for students to have real-world experiences and build important life skills.

Graduate education programs will find that this book gives specific and concrete information for the option of internships as part of experiential learning and high school reform.

We strongly believe in the power of internships to engage our young people and help them build the skills they will need for their future. We also believe that as educators we have an imperative to ensure that all our students are equipped for the challenges of the twenty-first century.

Acknowledgments

To Fred Koury, Richard Safran, and the original team that imagined and built City-as-School High School, NYC, and all those who kept true to Fred's vision through the years in spite of fads, panaceas, and mandates from above. The center has held. Thank you for believing.

A special thank you to Joan Chabrowe, CAS Resource Coordinator, who believed this book might be written one day and who still believes in the power of internships and to Nancy Dunwoody, without whom this book would have never made it onto the page.

Thank-you also to Dr. Mathew M. Mandery, director of the Nassau County High School Principals' Association Senior Year Network; Jay Lewis, Associate Dean, School of Education, Hofstra University; and Ms. Gene Silverman, executive director, Regional Schools and Instructional Programs, Nassau County, NY BOCES—for their continued work and belief in the power of a network to help schools establish senior projects.

A sincere thank-you to all of the teachers and administrators in the network, only some of whom are named here, who have built and sustained their programs and who took time to talk with us about their students and the importance of internships in helping them discover and reach their goals: Joseph Prisinzano, principal, Jericho High School, Jericho, NY; David Seinfeld, principal, Calhoun High School, Merrick, NY; Elizabeth McLaughlin and Danielle Casamassina, East Meadow High School, East Meadow, NY; Andrea Kaufman and Natalia McMillan, The Wheatley School, East Williston, NY; Russell Pajer, East Rockaway High School, East Rockaway, NY; Ilene Walker, Hewlett High School, Hewlett, NY; and Christopher Kauter, Deer Park High School, Deer Park, NY.

To all the MBA students in our classes at the University of Massachusetts-Dartmouth who have brought into the classroom their work experience and insights, helping us focus on the critical skills and competencies needed in today's world and ensuring that internships reflect the business challenges of the twenty-first century, we thank you.

A special thank-you to:

All administrators and teachers who worked to establish internship programs across the country, in schools large and small.

All interns who took a chance that they would learn more out in the real world.

The many business leaders, both here and in the UK, who believed in the value of an internship experience for our young people.

All those managers and supervisors in the many companies who have mentored and coached our young interns and built critical adult-to-adult relationships with them and helped them take firm steps into adulthood.

Additional thank-yous to:

Nancy Evans, acquisitions editor, and Carlie Wall, assistant editor, and Stephanie Sciuletti, associate editor, Rowman & Littlefield, for all their help and guidance.

Meghan and Matthew, for their patience and good humor while traipsing around the country to conferences and schools in support of internships.

And finally, a profound thank-you to Eugene P. Cimini, Esq., for his support and help in setting the lemonade stand.

Joan E. McLachlan
and
Patricia F. Hess

Introduction

Real-world experience really grounds students and school is no longer a theoretical hypothesis of what life will be like.

—Internship Sponsor [1]

TWENTY-FIRST-CENTURY INTERNSHIPS

Internships are critical for preparing our high school and community college students for life in the new economy. As the country moves from a manual, hands-on economy where most employees were involved with making things to a knowledge-based economy where more and more employees create value through their ideas, knowledge, and information management, students need to acquire the skills for success in this new world of work.

Technology plays an important part in this transition from a manual to a knowledge economy, freeing up the employee to create new products and services, question and improve the status quo, and find solutions to problems.

One way schools can play an important role in this transition, even in this time of limited resources, is to ensure that every student has the opportunity to participate in a quality internship. A quality internship has a robust curriculum focusing on building and strengthening academic and workplace skills, opportunities for the student to reflect and practice new skills in a safe environment, feedback from a variety of adults, and rigorous assessments that ensure that the student builds and develops the skills needed for today's workplace and further education.

Quality internships that are designed to include all students can level what is often an uneven playing field. Too often only certain students meet stringent criteria or have the connections and support to pursue an internship. This is usually truer for college level or post-college internships, but it can also occur on the secondary and community college level. Many students are not able to envision career possibilities because their own views have been limited. For them it is next to impossible to think of asking someone to be their internship sponsor without a great deal of support from adults around them. It is no wonder that these students often sign up for internships with relatives or neighbors in jobs that are not really of interest to them. Without help, they have no idea what is available in the word. This is where a developed, high-quality internship site can expand their horizons.

Traditionally internships have been a part of work-based learning. An internship is a partnership between the sponsoring business or organization and the school where the student gains valuable workplace experience and explores potential careers. The sponsor is an involved community participant, gets firsthand knowledge about potential employees, and strengthens the business/school connection. The goal of the internship is to provide a supervised learning experience in which students can apply their knowledge and build new skills in a real-world setting.

> Work-based learning has become familiar over the past 30 years as career exploration or school to work programs. It has several variants, such as job-shadowing, internships and full apprenticeships. It has been promoted by a variety of organizations: the Business Roundtable, the U.S. Department of Education, and Jobs for the Future in Boston. It has been a staple of career and vocational education. . . . Although most work-based learning programs are couched as partnerships between business or industry and a school, programs tend to seesaw between two competing interests: economic benefits to the business and personal benefits to the student.[2]

Students spend from a few weeks to a number of months in the work environment. The number of hours per week may vary according to the school and the placement. This placement may be with a for-profit company, a non-profit, educational or other organization. And the position may be paid or unpaid. While internships are most often unpaid, some schools and organizations may offer paid internships. However, schools that accept internship placements where the sponsor pays the student often find that the learning experience can become diluted. This is, in part, because the intern is viewed as an employee with tasks to complete rather than as a student who is there to learn and grow. The responsibility for student learning is with the school and the school needs to establish appropriate learning activities linked to curricula in partnership with the internship sponsor. This is more easily done when the intern is not paid. The school, however, may give credit for the internships as an elective that is often required for graduation. (See appendix for the U.S. Department of Labor's criteria for unpaid internships in the for-profit sector.)

The focus of the twenty-first-century internship must be on the quality of the learning experience in the workplace linked to the school curricula. Today's internships need to offer the student more than just work experience and career knowledge. Employers want evidence from job candidates that they are able to demonstrate problem solving, critical thinking, good communication, and teamwork. Organizations have become sophisticated in defining what these skills look like and expect recruiters to identify those candidates who are able to show practical evidence of them. And recruiters too have become more adept in uncovering a candidate's actual experience in using these skills.

Too often classroom exposure to these skills is not enough to get a candidate the job. However, students who have had an internship outshine others as they are able to give real-life examples of how they have tackled a problem, applied critical thinking to find a solution, tried a new approach to get results, and explained their work through self-confident communication. Students who are able to link their classroom learning to the real world are seen as having potential and are therefore in demand by an organization.

In today's economic climate employers and organizations are more demanding. They want candidates who have solid core skills in reading, writing, and math and they want candidates who are able to demonstrate twenty-first-century skills. The challenge to schools is to ensure that students have both the academic and practical life skills they need to be successful in the twenty-first-century workforce.

Research into today's economy indicates that students who are entering the workforce need more than only a high school education. The Center on Education and the Workforce at Georgetown University projects that the U.S. economy will create some forty-seven million job openings over the ten-year period ending in 2018 and that nearly two-thirds of these jobs will require that workers have at least some post-secondary education.[3] While some high school graduates want to enter the workforce immediately rather than continue with education after their graduation, there are many who look to a two- or four-year college program for additional educational or vocational qualifications.

Today's internships are one avenue for a school to ensure that all students have the knowledge and skills that make them attractive to employers whether they enter the workforce immediately from high school or community college or go on for further education and training. Internships give students the opportunity to test out a career before committing to studying for a specific qualification helps those students to broadly define their career interest and gain valuable life skills.

In addition, employers value real-world experience when they are hiring graduates of community colleges and universities. A *US News and World Report* survey indicates that employers want to hire those young people who have had an internship during their school and college career.[4]

While internships have been a part of work-based learning for the past thirty years, today's internships focus on ensuring that the student has the opportunity to develop specific skills so that she can successfully transition into the knowledge-based economy. Today's internships help the student build those transferrable skills that will lead to success in any job and in a variety of organizations. The twenty-first-century internship, whether in the for-profit or not-for-profit sector, enables the student to add value when she enters the workforce.

SKILLS FOR THE NEW ECONOMY

Much has been written about the skills needed in this new economy from an academic perspective. Internships in all fields provide students the opportunity to strengthen and apply their knowledge in language and communication for understanding, analysis and evaluation, and social interaction. Specific placements such as those in engineering, natural or agricultural sciences, and technology also give students opportunities to apply their knowledge in science and math. Seniors in high school and students in community college have proficiency in the foundation skills, and internships offer them a way to apply that knowledge in the real world. Tony Wagner, in a TED Talk, expressed the importance of being able to actually *use* skills:

> *The world doesn't care anymore what you know; all it cares is what you can do with what you know.*[5] *—Tony Wagner*

At the same time, organizations have invested their time and expertise in identifying those skills and behaviors that are needed for their leaders, managers, team leaders, and entry-level employees. These are often referred to as competencies and are written in behavioral terms. Although organizations may be for-profit or not-for-profit and in different sectors of the economy, many of the competencies are similar for entry-level jobs.

For example, organizations are looking for proficiency in:

- Written and oral communication
- Critical thinking and problem solving
- Teamwork and collaboration
- Motivation
- Personal awareness

Organizations are committed to these behaviors and often ask candidates for all levels of positions to show their awareness and experience in each. These skills and behaviors are not unique to any one organization or sector and are needed for both college and job success.

INTERNSHIPS MATTER

For the Student

An internship is a real-learning experience. Interns are not on their own but under the protective umbrella of the school or community college. Interns not only have the support of their school but are also able to ask their teacher for any help that they might need. Internships open the students to a new environment where they:

- Experience firsthand the world of work
- Gain an awareness of careers and career paths
- Have the opportunity to work on real-life projects that add value to a sponsoring organization
- Achieve measurable goals and complete activities in the real world
- Learn and practice the skills and behaviors expected in today's workplace
- Get feedback from teachers and workplace sponsors
- Build self-belief

Internships should be open to all high school and community college students. Real-world learning is not only for those students who are thinking about or planning on a specific or technical career but are increasingly valuable for students who are college bound and those who are unsure about what their work future may be.

Some schools offer internships as:

- An antidote for the "senior slump" for high school seniors, including those who have completed their academic requirements and are eager to get out into the real world as they wait for their graduation day
- An integrated part of their English, social studies, or business curricula, giving students an opportunity to apply their knowledge in the real world
- An intervention for students who may be at risk of dropping out and who would benefit from non-classroom learning
- An integrated part of the senior project
- An option in a community service or service learning program
- A pathway for special education students to transition from school to work
- An opportunity for all high school or community college students to gain firsthand experience in the real world

> We also need to elevate the critical importance of relevant work experience in a successful transition from adolescence to adulthood. The workplace is clearly the place to "try on" or test out a career choice. It is also by far the best venue in which to learn the "21st century skills" so critical to success in today's economy. And work linked learning can be extraordinarily powerful in engaging students who are bored or turned off by conventional classroom instruction.[6]

For the Sponsoring Organization

Although internships are structured as a learning experience for the student, organizations that take on or sponsor interns find that there are benefits for them. Interns generally want to be treated as entry-level employees and take on jobs and projects that the organization needs to have done.

- A positive internship experience encourages the intern to be an advocate for the organization with friends and family.
- By modeling the skills and behaviors required, organizations become an active participant in developing the future workforce in their community. Interns can learn new behaviors from getting to work on time to being a contributing member of a team.
- The supervisor or team leader of the organization often has the opportunity to manage, train, and coach the intern. This experience is a rich development opportunity that enables the employee to strengthen her management skills and move forward in her own career path.
- Partnering with local schools gives organizations enhanced visibility and enables them to build community support for their products and services.

QUALITY MATTERS

Today's changing economy is putting new demands on education to ensure that young people not only have a strong foundation in the academic subjects but are also able to

apply their knowledge in the real world. Many schools are showing a renewed interest in work-based learning so that students from middle school through high school
and community college are exposed to the world of work and to the new careers of
the twenty-first century. Internships, especially for high schools and community colleges, provide students with opportunities to translate their academic knowledge into
the real world and, at the same time, to build and strengthen the skills and behaviors
employers want.

However, for an internship to be of value to the student and the sponsor it needs
to be an integrated learning experience. Internships no longer can simply rely on an
attendance sheet to monitor the student and a student journal as the vehicle for reflective learning. Nor can a school assume that the sponsor is providing rigorous learning
opportunities for the intern to apply her knowledge and learn new skills.

Internships today must be structured so that the students know what is expected of
them as they meet the challenges of the work environment. Students also need to know
what success is and how it will be measured by the school and the sponsor. The school
needs to monitor and support the students in their placement. And sponsors need to
have the support from the schools as they work with the intern.

A quality internship program builds the skills required in the twenty-first century
and can be measured and sustained if the program has:

A Robust Curriculum

The curriculum in the form of a learning plan for the intern must focus on the development of the skills demanded for success in today's workplace. Each goal of an
internship learning plan needs to be aligned with building or strengthening specific
academic or workplace skills. Students need to know the specific goals and expected
outcomes. The school needs to monitor the student's learning through on-site visits,
telephone, Skype, and e-mail connections. This enables the school to guide and support the student and to stay in touch with the sponsor.

Reflection and Practice

An important part of a quality internship program is the opportunity for interns to reflect on their learning and experiences. Sharing of common experiences helps young
people gain insight into their own and others' behaviors. In addition, interns need a
safe place to practice and discuss their newly acquired skills. A weekly seminar, for
example, gives them a place away from the workplace to do this. But for maximum
learning, seminars need to be structured and facilitated.

Opportunity for Feedback

In the workplace, managers and supervisor routinely provide employees with feedback regarding their performance and behavior. Both positive and constructive feedback is necessary for an individual when she is learning new skills and behaviors. A
quality internship program ensures that there are a variety of adults who can provide
this feedback and act as mentors to the intern. The mentor is a guide or coach who

encourages and supports the intern as she is learning new skills. The mentor may be the intern's supervisor, the sponsor, teachers, and the internship coordinator.

Authentic Assessment

Students want to know how they have done in their internship. And teachers want to know what the student has learned. Performance-based assessments are an ideal way for the student to demonstrate what she has learned and for the teacher to have firsthand experience of this learning. Portfolios of the students' accomplishments help students organize their learning, including examples of specific work-related problems and how each was solved, evidence of actual work accomplished and the use of technology for research and written work. Structured presentations and exhibits enable the student to talk about her learning in front of others. These are excellent opportunities to involve sponsors and parents.

Five Essential Elements of Career Internship Programs [7]

- Concrete context for learning—the workplace
- Reflective context for learning—the integrative seminar
- One-on-one relationship for students with adult mentors
- Projects linking the seminar, the workplace, and academic disciplines negotiated among student, teacher, and supervisor
- Exhibitions and presentations of student work

Quality internship experiences in which students can show evidence of learning, give real examples of achieving goals, and demonstrate how their behaviors have changed are seen by potential employers and college admissions counselors as an indication of the student's ability to link classroom learning with the real world.

Ensuring that high school and community college students have the skills they need to be successful in the twenty-first-century workplace requires schools to do more than simply rely on extracurricular activities or part-time jobs to provide exposure to the workplace. It requires schools to offer a structured, challenging, and robust approach that ensures students have the experience they need to develop new skills and consolidate their classroom learning. Students need help and guidance to equip them for the challenges of the twenty-first century.

BUILDING SUSTAINABLE INTERNSHIPS

Many high schools and community colleges have limited time and resources to put career planning on the top of their agenda. Cutbacks in budgets and pressure from local, state, and federal governments requiring schools to focus on improving foundation skills leave little time to help students explore a variety of career options and to build the skills needed in today's workplace. And the workplace is rapidly changing. If teachers don't have a firsthand knowledge of how the workplace is different, it is difficult to equip students with the skills they need in this new environment.

Schools often shy away from implementing quality internship opportunities because they believe that this type of learning is not aligned with the necessary academic standards and that non-classroom learning is difficult to measure. Schools fear that internships are difficult to sustain from year to year and the use of their limited resources would be of more benefit if used elsewhere.

And yet internships can prepare students as they move into a career or higher education and are highly valued by employers.

Any school can start a quality, cost-effective internship program that can become the foundation needed to grow and sustain a challenging and robust program that prepares all students for the next stage of their life. A quality internship program is not difficult to start but it needs planning so that it is sustained from year to year.

> *Investments in work experiences for young adults will produce strong future returns.*[8]

TIPS ON STARTING AN INTERNSHIP PROGRAM

- *Start small*—Choose one class or a small group of students so that internships can easily be found and interns managed. Starting small also makes it easier to find and manage placement sites and build relationships with the employer sponsors.
- *Find a Champion*—A new program needs a Champion, someone who can talk about the value of the program to administrators, teachers, and students. This may be a faculty member or administrator who believes in the benefit of internships. This is the first step in getting buy-in from faculty, administrators, and sponsors.
- *Establish a budget*—While the cost of starting a small program can usually be found in the school's budget, addressing those costs early on will lay the foundation for building the program in the future.
- *Find placements and design the curriculum*—Based on the internships available, design the goals and activities suitable for each so that achievements can easily be measured.
- *Develop PR activities*—Stay connected with the employer sponsors and find opportunities for the students to talk about their learning and experience.

Once a program has been started, word of mouth by the interns often is the best PR. Interns not only enjoy their experience but also find that they have applied their knowledge in the real world and learned new skills.

However, as the program grows, the steps taken early on will ensure that the program maintains quality and is sustained from year to year:

- Ensure that internships are part of the culture of the school and not simply a project undertaken by one faculty member or class. The resources required, including the cost of the program director and materials, need to be part of the school's ongoing budget and not a grant. If the funding needed comes from a grant or special project the program runs the risk of not continuing once the grant money or project funds are no longer available.

- Widen the role of Champion to include others. Ensure that information about the program does not reside with only one person. While the program needs a Champion within the school, the information about sponsors, placements, interns, and curriculum needs to be available for others. Find opportunities for other faculty to be involved and add ideas. If only one faculty member has all the information about the program there is a danger that the internships will not be seen by others as integrated into the school's culture. If the person with all knowledge leaves, for any reason, the program could easily die.

- Publish the curriculum. A quality internship has learning plans for each intern, measurable goals and activities, and opportunities for the student to reflect and talk about his or her internship experience and learning. Learning plans can be amended and used year to year so that new ones do not need to be done for the same or similar placements. These plans should be open so that faculty members can give suggestions that might improve the intern's learning in their specific area.

- Keep statistics. As internships grow and more and more students want to participate in the program it is important to have quantifiable information. This can include numbers of interns, sponsors, cost, and attendance data. Having this data can show how the program is growing and also indicate that internships are an integrated part of the school's learning mission.

- Get feedback. Gather and record feedback from sponsors, interns, and faculty. Keeping this record will help shape the structure and learning plans for future participants. Asking for feedback sends a clear message that internships are part of the longer-term learning strategy for the school

- Continue to build PR. Develop PR plans so that sponsors and faculty continue to learn more about the value of internships. This will help employer sponsors to recommend other potential sponsors and the faculty will be reminded of the benefits of the internship experience.

- Use Technology. Find ways to use technology as part of the program and as a way to communicate to others about internships. Some schools integrate their internship program into the school's technology network so that all students know about it and interns can share their experiences with others. This promotes the program through the school even at younger grade levels.

Schools need to find ways to stay connected with the changes occurring in the workplace. Building relationships with sponsoring organizations can help teachers stay up-to-date. The global economy demands new skills. New technology requires new ways of thinking and working. Whether an internship is done for job preparation or for career awareness and experience it must be relevant to the changing economy. Sustainable quality internships ensure that students have the skills and knowledge that are needed for success as they move forward into the twenty-first century.

GOING FORWARD

The following chapters look at the specific components and structure of implementing and managing a quality internship program from start-up to establishing a sustainable program that ensures students are growing, personally and socially, as they develop and apply new skills and behaviors in a work environment. These chapters describe in detail all aspects of the quality internship program that will equip all students for the twenty-first-century world of work.

NOTES

1. Edutopia, "Real-World Internships Lead to College and Career Readiness," featuring MC2 STEM High School, Cleveland, Ohio. Edutopia Video, 6:38, February 27, 2013, www .edutopia.org/stw-college-career-stem-video.

2. Joseph DiMartino and John H. Clarke, *Personalizing the High School Experience for Each Student* (Alexandria, VA: Association for Supervision and Curriculum Development, 2008), 114.

3. Anthony P. Carnavele, Nicole Smith, and Jeff Strohl, *Help Wanted: Projections of Jobs and Education Requirements through 2018* (Washington, DC: Georgetown University: Center on Education and the Workforce, 2010), 13, www9.georgetown.edu/grad/gppi/hpi/cew/pdfs/FullReport.pdf.

4. Kimberly Palmer, "7 Things Employers Want from New Grads," *US News and World Report: Alpha Consumer* (web log), May 15, 2012, http://money.usnews.com/money/blogs/alpha-consumer/2012/05/15/7-things-employers-want-from-new-grads.

5. Tony Wagner, "Play, Passion Purpose. Independently Organized TED Event." TEDxNYED, 14:50. April 28, 2012. http://www.tedxtalks.ted.com/search/?=Tony+Wagner.

6. Harvard Graduate School of Education, *Pathways to Prosperity: Meeting the Challenge of Preparing Young Americans for the 21st Century*, report, Harvard Graduate School of Education, February 2011, www.gse.harvard.edu/news-impact/tag/pathways-to-prosperity.

7. Adria Steinberg, *Real Learning, Real Work: School-to-Work as High School Reform* (New York: Routledge, 1998), 83.

8. Harvard Graduate School of Education, *Pathways to Prosperity*, 25.

Chapter One

Key Elements of a Quality Internship Program

Getting It Right from the Start

A good internship challenges the student to use new knowledge to solve unfamiliar problems.

—Thomas R. Bailey[1]

A quality internship program needs resources, administrative support, and faculty commitment. Today many schools are financially stretched and find that they do not have the resources for a full-time faculty position to manage the program. Schools are often under pressure to use any additional resources to address academic needs, especially in reading and math.

However, if the key personnel in the school believe that real-world learning is a critical component of a young person's education so that they will have the opportunity to be successful in today's workplace, they need not put off starting a program because they can't assemble all of the components right away. Being aware of what a quality internship program includes will help the school build the components over time and the internship program will be contributing to the development of the twenty-first-century skills that are vital for our young people.

Internships can be set up in many different ways. Some are offered during the school day, some as summer work experiences, and some in the evening or on weekends. They can last for a few weeks, for the school semester or for the year—whatever the structure, a work experience can confirm, or rule out, a career choice. It can also help students cope with mistakes when the stakes aren't so high, as later in life.[2]

Whatever format a school chooses for their internship program, there are key elements that will ensure quality and success. This chapter focuses on those key elements that all quality internship programs have in common. Whether interns are students in secondary school or community college, all will benefit from a quality internship program.

WHAT NEEDS TO BE IN PLACE
BEFORE THE STUDENTS LEAVE THE BUILDING?

Before schools start thinking about the key elements of a quality internship program and how their program will implement them, there are some practical issues that need to be dealt with before even thinking of letting students leave the building. For schools starting out with no internship program at all, the first section of this chapter can serve as a guide to what needs to be discussed and decided upon before even thinking of sending teachers out of the building to develop internship sites.

There is one caveat we offer, based on past experience: *Write everything down.* If the internship program does not have documentation from the initial planning stages through the implementation of a pilot and any other programmatic revisions or expansions, much could be lost when personnel changes, programs and schedules change, or budgets are reconfigured. It is also useful to have documentation in the event that program information needs to be reported to the district, board, or administration.

As with any program developed in a school, one that will be designed to meet the particular needs of the students and community, every internship program needs the following.

A Vision and a Plan

Why have an internship program? What will the program look like? What students will be involved? Who will shepherd this new program through the development process? Where and when will the program operate? What are the goals and objectives? What is the basic description of the internship program? These are all questions that will come up during the planning process and it is best to figure out the answers at the beginning, rather than working backward, trying to fit in details at a later date.

Support

Without district- and building-level support, no program will get off the ground. If there is no buy-in at that level, any new program will have an uphill struggle. It may take some time to convince key players that an internship program is a worthwhile endeavor. If so, having the support of key parent and community members can often help. Providing research briefs also has helped in schools with administrations hesitant to get involved in internships. Buy-in at the school level is another issue. Some programs have been able to start with just a small core of supportive colleagues, building interest and additional support as the program grew and received positive feedback. It helps to keep in mind that it is not necessary to wait for total building-level support, because it probably won't happen.

Timeline

Once the team working on developing the internship program has dealt with the program's vision and gained support to go forward, it is time to set a realistic timeline.

If the lead-in is too long, people will get discouraged. If it is too short, important elements may get pushed aside and the quality of the program will suffer.

Deciding on who will do what, and a realistic time line until a pilot program can begin is critical for a successful program. It is also important to factor in the point at which students will begin to be involved in the program.

Administrative Issues

This is not the fun part of developing an internship program, but it is essential to get certain issues squared away while working on putting the rest of the program elements together.

Liability

This is probably the issue that most concerns schools when it comes to internship programs. And it should. However, it is not as difficult to deal with this issue as one may think. This book does not claim to offer legal advice. The information here is general and is included to stress the importance of consulting with the district's legal counsel to make sure all is in order around this issue.

Students in unpaid internship experiences cannot be covered by the employers' workers' compensation plan; however, because students' learning activities off school premises generally are considered to be an extension of the school, they are usually protected by the school district's liability policies. (See sample districts' hold harmless resolutions in the appendix.) Make sure these issues and policies are resolved with your board of education and legal advisors before placing any students. However, as more and more students take advantage of unpaid learning opportunities in the community, many employers and school administrators now want students covered by special insurance policies and riders. To provide this coverage a school district can amend its workers' compensation insurance or purchase separate medical coverage; also, an employer can acquire a general liability policy.

To avoid misunderstanding in the event of accident or injury, the employer and school contact should discuss all relevant insurance and liability issues before students enter the workplace. The school contact or administrator should get in touch with the district insurance agent or work through the board of education to determine specific provisions and call state and federal departments of labor to determine whether students are considered under the law to be in an employment relationship.

The sponsor should also be prepared to discuss liability issues with a representative of his or her insurance carrier to make sure all necessary coverage is in place. The school district and sponsor should sign a written agreement specifying the terms— such as insurance requirements, hold harmless statements, responsibility for supervision, and subrogation rights—of the liability and coverage for students.

Any school or district that was functioning during the school-to-work era probably already has the documents in place for students leaving the building for work-based trips, learning experiences, job shadowing, and group visits. The district's legal team needs to be consulted so that there are clear guidelines and required documents in place in this area.

Child-Labor Laws

Basically, child-labor laws do not apply if there is not an employment relationship; however, employers/sponsors are encouraged to adhere to child-labor laws with regard to hazardous conditions. No student should be placed in an internship with even the potential for hazardous conditions. School districts should be very careful here, and checking with the district's legal counsel is always recommended. The U.S. Department of Labor's Fact Sheet #71 addresses Internship Programs under the Fair Labor Standards Act and is included in the appendix.

Transportation

In general, liability for injuries or accidents during transit rests with the party responsible for transportation. For example, a student is responsible if he or she drives a personally owned car; the district is responsible if students travel by school transportation; and the employer is responsible if students are transported in a company-owned vehicle. There are, however, variations in different districts and states, making it necessary for the school contact, working with the sponsor and school district, to determine the standards that apply locally. This is another item to discuss with the district's counsel.

In addition to the legal issues around student transportation, many schools encounter difficulties with finding ways for students to get to and from their internship placements. One school reported that their belief was that if the students could get to the mall on weekends, they could get to internship placements—and this seemed to work for the majority of their students. In districts where students arrive on buses, often the buses, when not used during the day, can be used to pick up and drop off students along an agreed-upon route if there is no public transportation. If there is, often transit passes can be obtained at low or no cost to the school. Many times, parents are willing to help their students get to and from an internship. Students also drive their own cars or use bicycles and even walk if the school and/or their homes are not too far from the internship placement. There is one caution, however, about students using their own cars. Consult the district's legal counsel about the issue of students transporting other students in private cars. The regulations around this situation need to be made very clear to all concerned.

Funding

Before an internship program can be a reality, it needs to be part of the school curriculum, either as a freestanding program or as an integrated part of an existing class. The time for the coordinator to spend in internship duties is often built into that teacher's program and thus the program is funded by part of a teacher's regular program. Grants can help start programs, but programs that are sustainable cannot expect to run on the unpredictable soft money of grants.

Granting of Credit

This aspect of an internship program needs to be decided before students are even recruited to the program. They need to know if their work will result in credits on their transcript, credits toward work in a connected class, or any other way credits might be awarded. The type and amount of credit awarded also need to be established so there is no misunderstanding in the future.

Scheduling Personnel and Students

Because scheduling usually involves the guidance department, it is helpful to involve a member of this department in the initial planning phase. This is an aspect of an internship program that needs to be worked out with the building administration too as some schools have tried to schedule internships early in the day, only to learn that businesses don't usually want students on-site at 8:00 a.m. or earlier. Prime time for internships is in the afternoon when students often have a light program, but again, the master school schedule is affected if a group of students needs to be free to leave the building in the early afternoon. The internship coordinator needs to have time in the afternoon to visit sites and this can impact the school schedule.

Personnel

As the program planning moves along, the determination of who will be in charge, what other personnel and support staff will be needed, and what part the guidance department and other professional staff will play should be clarified and time for their participation in the internship program should be an official part of their duties.

Technology and Office Support

Because an internship program deals constantly with the world outside of the school, it is critical that the people who work in the program have access to telephones (direct outside lines and cell phones), faxes, copiers, and dedicated computers with e-mail accounts specifically for the internship program. Interns and sponsors need to be able to contact the coordinator easily, and going through a school switchboard or using a teacher's personal e-mail is not adequate.

Forms Related to Internships

Listed below are many of the forms related to internships that should be in place:

- Memorandum of agreement
- School or district liability form
- Internship activity curriculum packet
- Logs or journal forms
- Attendance forms
- Warning notices
- Reporting or date due schedule based on site curriculum
- Sponsor evaluation forms
- Student evaluation forms
- Year/semester calendar (with school holidays) for sponsor and students

- Plan for assessment
- Method for reporting internship on school transcript, college application, and résumé

Once the basics of establishing the framework of a new or revamped internship program are completed, it is time to work on the elements that will make it a high-quality program.

These elements are listed below, included on the figure 1.1 checklist, and are discussed in detail in subsequent chapters.

- Assessing the community for potential internships and internship site development
- Selection and placement of students and orienting students to internships
- In-school reflective seminars or class to support internships
- Monitoring and assessment of internships (both student's progress and site's)
- Plan for public relations activities

Having a checklist can help in keeping track of the elements of the internship program that have already been dealt with and those that still need to be addressed.

Research and experience have indicated not all internship opportunities provide powerful experiences and learning. Quality internships enable students to reflect new experiences and enable supervisors and teachers to tease out new knowledge and insight. Good internships bring more adults into the lives of young people and help young people to engage with the world outside of school in compelling ways and encourage them to develop new reserves of self-respect and social skills.[3]

QUALITY INTERNSHIPS

A quality program needs to be structured, monitored, and focused on the student, school, sponsor, and community. Solid programs have specific learning goals and outcomes for the student, opportunities to reflect on learning, opportunities to practice new skills, opportunities for feedback, and robust assessment. Quality programs also have clearly defined roles for the adults involved as well as for the student intern. A clear program structure helps the student to get the most value from his internship experience and ensures student success.

No matter what the setting, a quality internship program has common elements for the students, the school, the sponsor, and the community. Programs that are sustainable and measurable have several key elements in common.

A quality internship program takes into consideration the needs of all involved in the program.

What Students Need

Quality Placements

Students need a choice of quality placements not just an assignment in one place. This would mean that adults would have to find more than one placement and develop each

KEY ELEMENTS OF A QUALITY INTERNSHIP PROGRAM:
What Needs to Be in Place before Students Leave the Building?

☐   A Vision And A Plan
      Why have an internship program?
      Agreement on Goals and Objectives
      Program Description
      What will program look like?
      Who? (students and staff)
      Where? (housed)
      When? (hours, time)

☐   Support
      Administrative—District and building level
      Building Level Colleagues
      Community and Parental

☐   Timeline
      When and who will do what?
      When will pilot/program begin?

☐   Administrative Issues
      Liability   Funding
      Child Labor Laws   Granting of Credit
      Transportation   Scheduling personnel and
                      students

☐   Personnel
      Who will be in charge?
      What other personnel is needed?
      Guidance
      Other Professional Staff to be involved

☐   Technology and Office Support
      Access to:
        Telephones   Copier
        Fax   Computers

Figure 1.1. Key Elements of a Quality Internship Program: What Needs to Be in Place before Students Leave the Building?

☐	**All Forms Related to Internships** Memorandum of Agreement School or District Liability Form Internship Activity Curriculum Packet Logs or Journal forms Attendance forms Warning notices Reporting/dates due Sponsor Evaluation Forms Student Evaluation Forms Year/semester calendar (with school holidays) Plan for Assessment Method for reporting Internship on school transcript, college application, resume
☐	Assessing the Community for Potential Internships—Discussed in detail in Chapter 2.
☐	Internship Site Development—Discussed in detail in Chapter 2.
☐	Selection and Placement of Students—Discussed in detail in Chapter 3.
☐	Plan for Monitoring and Assessment of Internships (Both Students' Progress and Site)—Discussed in detail in Chapters 4 and 7.
☐	Plan for In-School Reflective Seminars or Class—Discussed in detail in Chapter 6.
☐	Plan for Public Relations Activities (To Build Program Support) Brochures News articles Recognition Ceremonies for Sponsors Student Presentation Fair

Figure 1.1. (*continued*)

as a proper site. This might be hard in a small community, but usually there are at least two places that would qualify if people look hard enough. Chapter 2 discusses the development of internship sites and shows the variety of placements available in even the smallest of communities.

Placements need to be noncompetitive so that students do not have to compete with one another to get the good placements. This is a learning experience, not a contest. Students who are not as outgoing (or pushy) as other students can end up not getting the internship they need or want because they are not used to stepping up. At the secondary school or community college level, students often still need assistance in this area. There will be time enough for competition in the years to come.

Placements need to be vetted by a teacher or internship coordinator to make sure that it is not just a "gofer" placement and to make sure that it is safe, both inside and out (site and neighborhood). If the coordinator feels the placement is not in a safe area, considering that students often will be leaving the placement after dark in the winter months, then another placement needs to be found.

Curriculum

A curriculum or guide is needed so that the student knows what he or she should be doing and learning. Doing and learning are two different things. The main questions the adult has to ask are "What can a student *do* here, and what can a student *learn* here?" The curriculum needs to be something much more than a journal. It is here that the teacher and the sponsor can work together to answer these questions and develop a learning plan for the intern. Sample curriculum packets (Internship Learning Plans) are included in this book in the appendix.

Supervision and Direction

Students need one person to report to both on-site and in the school setting. Otherwise students get lost in the shuffle and the internship can unravel. Usually it is the internship coordinator who is in charge of this aspect of the program. Ideally an orientation session is held or an orientation book is provided to each intern so that everyone is on the same page and the coordinator doesn't have to repeat instructions and details over and over.

Students also need an orientation to the entire internship site and specifically the "local" department where the student will be working. Students need to know where they are, especially in an unfamiliar place.

In terms of day-to-day functioning, the intern needs to be very clear about how to handle absences, school holidays, and other issues of attendance.

Most importantly, the intern needs to know that there is one person from the school who is the go-to person for guidance and any problems that may crop up. This person needs to have time to visit the student to talk about and observe progress and to give the student a chance to demonstrate learning.

Seminar

Seminar time for "debriefing" and reflecting about the internship experience in school is key to helping students understand their internship experiences. This is the opportunity for the student to consolidate his learning from the internship experience. Seminars should be conducted by someone who is familiar with what the student is supposed to be doing out in the field. Many schools use part of a class period for seminar time. Some are able to schedule a specific period for this activity. A great deal of learning at an internship is lost if students do not have a dedicated time to reflect on what they are doing and learning.

Mentor

The mentor is the person who is able to provide experience and reinforce learning on a one-to-one basis. He or she may be the sponsor, workplace supervisor, or someone from the school's established mentoring program. A mentor is another adult connection for the young person.

Culminating or Capstone Experience

The importance of a culminating experience at the completion of the placement cannot be stressed enough. This is the time when the student reflects on their experience and learning and helps to connect the real world with what they have done in school and is key to success. This may be in the form of a presentation to an audience of teachers, other students, sponsors, and even parents and other relatives. It may also take the form of an exhibit. Some schools have full-blown exhibition fairs featuring interns, and others have students present their internships during class time. A very important learning opportunity is missed when internship programs simply end without some type of capstone activity.

Evaluation and Feedback

An opportunity for feedback or assessment is a key learning experience for students. Students want to know how they have done in their internship experience and if they will be given credit. An assessment of the student's work and achievement that can be presented in the form of a portfolio will help the student to see the relevance of the experience to his or her future. A student presentation or exhibit enables the students to talk about their experience and learning.

What the School and Internship Program Need

Structure

Quality internships need structure. And it is the school, through teachers and coordinators who develop the structure, which enables the opportunity for real-world learning to occur. Structure also ensures that the school knows what learning is occurring during the internship experience. The school needs to make sure that there are:

An Internship Coordinator (and Support Staff)

Every program needs someone who is in charge and is the point person. This individual needs to be accountable for the smooth running of the program. This is the person to whom teachers and administrators can ask questions and get straight answers.

This person may be a coordinator or teacher who can also act as the site supervisor who visits the students in their placement on a regular basis. In this visit the site supervisor monitors the learning, talks to the student about progress and problems, confers with the sponsor, mediates any problems, and gives the student an opportunity to demonstrate learning. This visit also helps the sponsor or to stay connected with the school.

The coordinator may also be the person to place the students in their sites and make sure that the curriculum or learning plan is in place. This is especially important at the start of a program when sponsors are new and internships are new to the school.

Seminar or Classroom Opportunities

Seminars or classroom opportunities and the mentoring schedule could also be the responsibility of the internship coordinator or another person in the school. This individual could conduct the seminars or reflection time or ensure that there are appropriate teachers available to do so. It is at these seminars that the students begin to connect their real-world learning with their classroom learning.

Internship Standards and Expectations

Standards, expectations, and assessment guidelines, which are clear and communicated to the students before the start of any internship experience, are critical. A quality internship program that is structured, has clear standards and expectations, and is easy to implement enables the school to strengthen the learning links between the classroom and the real world.

What Sponsors Need

To Feel Valued

Sponsors want to feel that they are making a difference in a young person's life. They also want to feel that they are contributing, in some way, to the young person's education and skill building. In so doing, they want to stay connected with the school. And they need feedback and support throughout the internship experience.

Regular Contact

The most important aspect of this connection is having one person as the contact point in the school for the sponsor to contact. An e-mail address that will be responded to and a cell phone or direct line to the coordinator are critical for continuing sponsor support. If a sponsor has to call the school's main office and gets passed from desk to desk and then has to leave a message with someone who has no idea who is calling or why, extreme frustration can follow.

Regular visits and contact by phone and e-mail by the teacher/coordinator help to ensure that any problems are identified early and that the sponsor does not feel unsupported by the school. Sponsors also appreciate help with an orientation guide to their site.

Curriculum Specific to the Internship Site

Sponsors want to be involved in what the intern is doing and learning. A site-specific learning plan with sponsor input in the development of the plan or in amendments to an existing plan is vital.

To Be Kept in the Loop

The sponsor needs to know from the school about any attendance requirements for the student, the school's calendar, and holidays. Businesses do not operate on school time and some find the frequent days off, half days, closings, and testing schedules very confusing. Sponsors also need to be aware of any forms the student has, such as emergency medical contact information.

Sponsors also need to know that students are prepared for their work experience and that they have had some type of orientation to the internship experience.

Recognition

Recognition is a key element and contributor to whether or not an individual sponsor continues to support the program and take interns in the future. A breakfast for sponsor and interns, signs designating them as sponsor sites for the school, and certificates are some ways schools can say, "Thanks for your support and contributing to a young person's future." Schools need to publicly recognize their sponsors in local newspaper articles and through the chamber of commerce and other community organizations. An internship program is the public face of the school and making sure relationships outside the school building are respected and recognized is good public relations for the district and a way to help the internship program grow.

What Parents and the Community Need

To Know What Is Going On and What to Expect

Parents need to know how to contact the school, not the internship site, if there is a problem with their son or daughter. Businesses will deal with schools but they don't want to deal with parents.

Student presentations and/or exhibits are an excellent opportunity for the school to invite parents to learn about the internship in which their students have participated.

The community needs to know what is going on. Some people are nervous when they see teens out in the community during school hours. Schools need to get out the word that their students are doing internships. This will show the larger community that there is a connection between school and work so that other sponsors will volunteer to be part of the program.

It is helpful to keep a checklist (see figure 1.2) of the key elements for a quality internship program available as an internship program is planned and implemented. That way the team working on the program can be aware of the components that still need to be addressed.

Checklist for Quality Internships

What Students Need	
☐	Quality Placement
	__ A Choice of Placements Not just an assignment to one place. This might be hard in a small community, but usually there are at least two places that would qualify if people look hard enough. __ Non-Competitive Placement Students shouldn't have to compete with one another to get the good placements. This is a learning experience, not a contest.
☐	A Curriculum
	__ Learning guide to what the student should be doing and learning. Doing and learning are two different things. The main questions the adult has to ask the sponsor are "what can a student DO here and what can a student LEARN here?" Something much more than journals and an attendance sheet are needed.
☐	Supervision and Direction
	__ One person to report to both on-site and in the school setting. Otherwise students get lost in the shuffle and internships unravel. __ An orientation to internships in general the specific site where the intern will be working. __ A simple system for reporting and dealing with absences. Schools need a formal record and so does the sponsor __ A field supervisor from the school to VISIT the student on a regular basis and to talk about progress and problems…to confer with the sponsor…to mediate problems….and to give the student a chance to demonstrate learning. Often interns labor in isolation and quickly lose interest when no one is there to see what they are doing
☐	Seminar
	__ Seminar for "debriefing" and reflecting about the internship experience in school conducted by someone who is familiar with what the student is supposed to be doing out in the field
☐	Mentor
	__ A role for the sponsor or other adult to provide experience and reinforce learning on a one-to-one basis

Figure 1.2.   Checklist for Quality Internships

☐	Culminating or Capstone Experience
	__ A Capstone experience or presentation time with an audience—something to have the student reflect on what they have been doing and learning and help them connect it with what they've done in school and what they will be doing in the future.
☐	Evaluation and Feedback
	__ An opportunity for feedback or assessment is a key learning experience for interns.

What the School and Internship Program Need	
☐	Structure
	__ The internship program needs a clear vision of who and what it is for, how it will be operated, and who will be in charge.
☐	Internship Coordinator and support staff (This person could do all the jobs listed below, or the duties could be shared with colleagues.)
	__ Someone to be in charge and be the point person. __ Someone to place the students. __ Someone to make sure there is a curriculum packet in place for each internship. __ Someone to regularly visit the interns at the sites to check on progress. __ Someone to read and review all the assignments. The sponsor can do this too, but the ultimate responsibility rests with the school. Why should a student write something if no one is going to read it? __ Someone to supervise and organize the capstone activity. __ Someone to look for and develop new internship sites. Sites can go stale and so can the people in them. __ Someone to conduct public relations activities. Schools need to get out the word that their students are doing internships and that internship sites are needed. __ Someone to help publicly recognize sponsors in the community.
☐	Seminar or Classroom Opportunities
	__ Someone to conduct the weekly seminars for students to reflect on what they are doing in their internships and how it is connected to what they are doing in school and will do in the future.
☐	Internship Standards and Expectations
	__ It is critical to establish standards, expectations, and assessment guidelines, which are clear and communicated to the students before the start of any Internship experience.

Figure 1.2. (*continued*)

What Sponsors Need	
☐	To Feel Valued
☐	Regular contact with the school
	__ Contact with one school person __ Regular visits and phone contact with the school __ Help with an orientation guide from the school
☐	Curriculum specific to their site __ Help with designing activities for the student to do.
☐	To be kept in the loop __ Forms from school for attendance, and school calendar, so they know holidays, and knowledge that students have been prepared though an orientation
☐	Recognition for their work __ A simple thank you __ A breakfast for sponsors with their interns; signs designating them as sponsor sites for XYZ School; certificates
What Parents And Communities Members Need	
☐	__ To know how to contact the school—NOT THE INTERNSHIP SITE if there is a problem with their son or daughter. Businesses will deal with schools, but they dislike dealing with parents. The fastest way to lose an internship site is to have hovering parents interfering.
☐	__ To know what is going on. Some people are nervous when they see teens wandering in the community during school hours.

Figure 1.2. (*continued*)

NOTES

1. Thomas R. Bailey, Katherine L. Hughes, and David Thornton Moore, *Working Knowledge: Work-based Learning and Education Reform* (New York: Routledge, 2004), 221.

2. Caralee J. Adams, "Internships Help Students Prepare for Workplace," *Education Week*, January 30, 2013, Focus On: Career Readiness, www.edweek.org/ew/articles/2013/01/30/19internship_ep.h32.html?tkn=RRZFP0oFcFfP12gPvr+6KdgwXa6W4oXc5RPD.

3. Bailey, Hugues, and Moore, *Working Knowledge*, 222.

Chapter Two

Internship Site Development
Internships Don't Just Happen

The belief that all genuine education comes about through experience does not mean that all experiences are genuinely or equally educative.

—John Dewey[1]

The foundation of a good internship program, one that does not require extra time duplicating efforts, is a reliable collection of placement sites that have been developed in the most efficient way possible. Too often those charged with developing sites have had to make several follow-up phone calls or visits because the needed information was not obtained or shared with the sponsor during the first visit.

For ease of understanding, this chapter is divided into three sections:

Section One—*Finding Community Internship Sponsors* discusses ways to go about locating possible internship sites in the community.

Section Two—*Developing Internship Sites* focuses on a logical approach to developing those sites, including how to conduct the initial visit or telephone interview with the sponsor, the most important items to cover during the discussion, what the school expects of the sponsor, what the school's role will be, and the importance of the Internship Learning Plan.

Section Three—*Developing the Internship Learning Plan* discusses the writing of the Internship Learning Plan for each site.

The appendix to this book includes examples of documents referred to in this chapter.

SECTION ONE—FINDING COMMUNITY INTERNSHIP SPONSORS

Every Community Has Potential Internship Sites

One of the first conversations most schools have about establishing an internship program is around availability—or perceived nonavailability—of internship sites.

"Where will we find placements? We aren't a big city. There is nothing interesting here" are some of the first comments when talk turns to internships. Some schools stop right there, convinced that their community is not one that could provide any, let alone quality, internship experiences. Those that keep the conversation going eventually realize that practically every community has something to offer students wishing to learn in the real world. If educators are willing to dig into what actually happens in a business or organization and are willing to help students see what can be learned there, then internship sites can be developed.

Internship programs have been established in sites as diverse as suburbs, college towns, small cities, rural locations, and even a school for court-remanded youth situated in the middle of nowhere. Wherever people work, students can learn. Every community has small businesses, museums, or historical sites no matter how small and seemingly insignificant. Most communities have hospitals, clinics, or professional offices, craftspeople, farmers or florists, theaters or other arts organizations, printers or graphic artists, non-profit organizations, elected officials' local offices, and government agencies. Schools themselves also provide placements for students to serve as tutors and assistant teachers. Student interns can even assist in setting up the initial internship program.

How Can a School Find Internship Sponsors?

Everyone is a possibility! Everyone works or knows someone who works. Networking with friends, neighbors, relatives of staff, and students is a good place to begin. If there is an existing internship program or work-based learning program in the district, use referrals from existing sites.

Sometimes organizations like Rotary, local business organizations, or the chamber of commerce can be a source of referrals. Keep in mind however that each site still needs to be developed one by one as each site is unique in some way and not all sites will be interesting to or appropriate for all students.

Use mailings. This is best used after the program is established. Personal contact is the best way to get a program off the ground. Make phone calls. (Use the online directories if nothing else works. Once the program is established and people start calling, cold calls will be unnecessary.)

Probably the best way to identify potential internship sites is to brainstorm with colleagues. A little time spent brainstorming with colleagues can bring surprising results in listing possibilities to pursue.

The Community Assessment Form (figure 2.1) illustrates the types of possible internship sites a community may have available. A blank form similar to this will help get brainstorming started.

Are there golf courses near the school? There is much more to golf than swinging a club. There are possibilities for learning about the ecological issues of maintaining the course, or the history of golf, or the evolution of rules and the physics of ever-improving equipment.

If an antique store is part of the community, there are opportunities for experiences in small business operations, bookkeeping, customer service, merchandising, advertising, history (local, state, and national).

Community Assessment Form

Personal Connections	Community/Neighborhood Related	Small and Local Businesses
Dr. Smith - Vet	Three Rivers Social Services	Richardson Floral
Tom Jacobs - Architect	Veterans' Peace Center	Corner Business Center
Pets R Us Groomers	A Baby Place	Webb's Web Design
Wildlife Rescue Center	Smithfield Allergy Clinic	Local Service Station
Dr. Filmore, DDS	Schools/Day Care	Senior Center Food Services
Jim's uncle - Accounting firm	Newspapers	Garden Designers

COMMUNITY RESOURCES FOR INTERNSHIPS

Government (Local, State, Federal)	Large National Businesses and Industries	Artists / Crafts persons / Musicians
Mayor Jefferson	ACME Industries	Stained Glass Gallery
Congressional offices - Smith, Edwards	GE Diesel	Mountain Potters
State Senator Gates	Banks	Northern Furniture Crafters
Water Dept.	Hotels and Conference Centers	Arts for All - Classes and individual instruction
County Commission	Regional Manufacturing Center	Music Masters Music School

© 2013 *Internship Quest, LLC.*
Reprinted courtesy of Internship Quest, LLC.   www.internshipquest.com

Figure 2.1.   Community Assessment Form

Most towns have grocery stores and service stations. Cashiers, stockers, and clerks are the people seen "out front" at these businesses. But behind the scenes there are many possibilities for learning about economics, current events affecting the businesses, industry information, supply and demand principles, logistics, and transportation.

Once possible sponsors are identified, then comes the up-front work for every internship program. Developing a quality internship site does take time initially, but it is worth the work because a well-developed site can serve many students through the years, with just minor adjustments, from time to time, to the learning goals attached to that site. Some programs start out enthusiastically with students locating and basically developing their own internship experiences and setting their own goals. This method seems to work well for students who are self-motivated and have support from family and others, and appear to know in what direction they want to go, but it doesn't work so well for those students who need more support, and need help seeing possibilities and options and assistance making connections. Plus it is very time-consuming for the educator responsible for overseeing many students going in many directions with various formats for their Internship Learning Plans.

Every internship site needs a carefully written Internship Learning Plan attached to it, one that has uniform goals (discussed next) and suggested, but flexible, learning goals and activities. This allows the school to keep a collection of internship site learning plans to draw on when the program is gaining speed and students. To have to stop and list goals and activities or review student-designed goals and activities for every possible intern each semester or quarter can be very time-consuming. And it leaves very little time for the internship supervisor to actually spend time helping to match students to a proper internship, supervise that student, and help the student reflect on what can be beneficial to them, not just in their internship area but in all aspects of life beyond secondary school.

SECTION TWO—DEVELOPING INTERNSHIP SITES

While considering and developing internship sites, these two questions should be kept in mind:

What can a student *do* at this site?

What can a student *learn* at this site?

The site developer/internship coordinator needs to ask: What can a student *learn* at or from a quarry, a cemetery, a little theater, an insurance company, a real estate office, a potter's studio, a nursing home, a brickyard, a house painter, a local elected official, the town water department? And then, the most important question needs to be asked: What can a student *do* at these places? If the answer is: observe, follow people around, listen in, make copies, keep the coffee going and run errands, then a different site needs to be found.

The questions above will be the two main questions that need to be answered when talking with the sponsor and setting up the internship site. Additional questions to keep in mind are:

• Does the program need a placement in this area? As much as every business or organization may seem appealing, some are just not going to give students that much useful experience or help in exploring career possibilities.

Examples of Suitable and Unsuitable Internship Sites

During one site visit to a school in New England, we visited three possible sponsors:

One was a bagpipe maker for a police department. Although this was very interesting and unique, the decision was made that this might not be a great career opportunity for a student in the future.

Another, a coffee importer, at first seemed like a possibility for a great deal of learning. However, a short discussion revealed that the actual buyers were rarely in the office or facility and were interested mainly in clerical help, and the only person who would be there on a regular basis would be an office assistant who had no interest in having an intern around.

The last office visited in the building was that of a pediatric dental clinic. Jackpot! They were interested in having an intern. There were a great many tasks the intern could actually perform and a great deal to learn, and several of the adults working there were interested in having a young person explore their various career areas—all of this in one office.

- Do the possible activities match student interest and abilities?
- Is the location safe and accessible?
- Will there be regular supervision?
- Will students have tasks that are interesting and meaningful and not just monotonous?
- Does the potential sponsor understand that student interns are not "gofers" or free labor?
- Is this potential site in a career area that will be beneficial to an intern in the long run?

The community internship sponsors willing to work with students in a career environment must agree with the school's internship philosophy that the focus of the student's experience must be on learning, and the internship sponsor must be willing to work with school program staff to develop curriculum to further that learning.

After a few brainstorming sessions with colleagues, it's time to begin to actually develop internship sites. Start by listing those businesses and organizations that are most likely to be interested in serving as sponsors. The development of a sponsor site should follow a logical sequence so nothing gets left out and work doesn't have to be duplicated.

The Initial Visit

Call the potential sponsor, explain a bit about the program (a printed script may help here), and ask to make an appointment to visit. The visit shouldn't take more than forty-five minutes. Keep in mind that people are very busy and making more time for a visit may be very difficult. The site developer needs to practice getting the needed information as quickly as possible. Teachers don't have all that much time either.

In reality, do all internship programs initially have someone visit every internship site? Probably not. Ideally each site should be visited and each sponsor should be personally interviewed, but realistically, sometimes there is no time for that. However, keep in mind that the school will be sending students to this location and therefore someone needs to make sure that it is safe, clean, accessible, and staffed by reliable people who know what the internship program is all about and what is expected of them as a sponsor. If an initial visit cannot be made, a telephone interview might substitute if this contact has been made through a reliable contact or colleague.

What to Take on Internship Development Visits

The initial visit is an opportunity both to communicate the program's educational standards and to establish personal rapport. Make sure to take the following:

- Listing of other internships (if available)
- The program brochure or some descriptive piece even if it is just a nicely word-processed one-pager

- Examples of Internship Learning Plans (use the examples from the appendix of this book if there are none developed yet)
- Internship Development Form filled out by this organization in response to the initial contact plus extra Internship Development Forms. Sometimes this is filled out at the first visit in smaller locations.
- Forms that the program will use regularly: attendance, letter of introduction, end-of-internship student and sponsor evaluations, semester calendar, and emergency contact form
- District Liability Statement (see appendix)

Example of a Completed Internship Site Development Form

Title:	*Ecology Intern*
Internship Site:	*Marshland Conservation Society*
Address:	*123 Smith Street*
	Our Town, MA 10000
Telephone:	*(555) 434-1111*
Fax:	*(555) 434-1110*
Email:	*director@marshland.org*
Sponsor Name:	*Martin Smith, Arnold Jones*
Internship Coordinator:	*Carol Reed*

Description: *This learning plan can be used for a local government conservation or natural resources department, a non-profit conservation project, a local environmental students department or local museum of natural history.*

General Responsibilities: *Marshland Conservation Society. This is an opportunity for the intern to learn about the marshland, how our ecosystem works, how the marshland habitat sustains the fish, birds and other animals of the region. It is also an opportunity for the intern to communicate to others the challenges facing marshland preservation. The intern will help administratively, do at least one research project, and lead tours of the facility.*

This is an ideal internship for students who are interested in our environment, want to conserve wildlife habitat and/or who want to work outside.

Figure 2.2.   Example of a Completed Internship Site Development Form

What to Cover on the Internship Development Visits

- The sponsor needs to know the intent and goals of the school's program, and some background and outcomes expected.
- The sponsor will also want to know how students are placed and their role in any interview process.
- Guidelines and expectations about attendance, attire, completion of the Internship Learning Plan, expected behavior, and school and internship site rules and regulations.
- The sponsor's responsibilities in case of a problem or an accident.
- Provision for lunch and transportation. (Although student interns usually earn no salary, some large companies provide lunch in the company cafeteria or from petty cash. This is especially important if the school has a large Title I population.) Some schools have arranged for cafeterias to provide box lunches for students leaving from school.
- Sponsors also need to be reminded that working with adolescents can be challenging at times. Many people do not have teenage children, have not been around adolescents a lot, and do not remember their own adolescence fondly. It helps to remind them that adolescents face many challenges in their journey to adulthood. Although they are eager for opportunities to make decisions, they are also uneasy with the consequences of those decisions.
- Sponsors benefit from a gentle reminder that adolescents want to try out different values and build their own philosophies. They want respect from adults—although they may feign indifference and very often they have feelings of insecurity in new settings with adults, even though they put on an air of confidence. In their desire for independence and privileges they may have trouble with responsibility and personal discipline. And most shocking to many business people, is that adolescents are very interested in physical appearance—their own standard, not an adult's. This can create big conflicts at an internship if not dealt with up front.

Although the school should provide an orientation that includes what to expect at an internship, including best bets for attire, the sponsor needs to be reminded to make the office dress policy clear before a problem arises. It helps if a sponsor has a formal orientation for the intern that includes standards.

What Does the School Expect the Sponsor to Provide?

There are some basic things a student needs at an internship site.

- Supervision and a safe learning environment
- An understanding that a student in an internship experience is not a paid employee and that the main goal is student learning
- An understanding that credit is being earned for specific responsibilities (if this is a credit-bearing internship) outlined in the Internship Learning Plan
- Support and work with the student in completing the Internship Learning Plan
- A work area or desk for the student

Overall, the sponsor is expected to provide leadership and motivation for the student and to be clear when delegating and communicating expectations. The sponsor also is expected to help with the intern's development and training at the internship site and to evaluate performance at the end of the internship.

What Can the Sponsor Expect from the School?

It is important to stress to the potential sponsor that the school will always be available for any needed support, that regular contact by phone, e-mail, and visits can be expected, and that there is a specific person to call if needed. They also need to know that the student will be receiving support from the school and that the sponsor does not have to be solely in charge of everything.

Preparing to Write the Internship Learning Plan

Keeping a record of every site developed and the Internship Learning Plan developed for the site will save time in the future if another student is interested in interning at this site.

For every site, create a folder with the name and contact information for the sponsor (and the internship code if one will be used). All future records (Internship Learning Plans, correspondence, reports on visits, attendance sheets, etc.) for this sponsor will be placed here. Complete the initial site visit forms and place them in the folder for future reference. Write a description and preliminary Internship Learning Plan. Mail, e-mail, or fax them to the sponsor for review.

Develop a procedure for adding new internship sites to the master list or catalog and add each one as it is developed. Standardizing the format and method for listing available internships will save time and trouble later.

Begin to write notes and a description of the site using the Internship Site Development Form (figure 2.2). This will be used for the Internship Learning Plan and for future reference and can save a great deal of time and ensure that important points are not overlooked.

Use the Internship Development Form for making revisions when there is a change in address, personnel, etc. If everything is standardized, then others will not have difficulty if the program expands, is turned over to another person, or if the recordkeeping is taken over by a secretary or assistant.

If it is decided to code the internships, deal with the school's guidance department at the beginning to set up a system everyone can understand and one that can be used by computer programs.

What If the Site Is Not Suitable for the Program's Students?

If, after a visit to a sponsor, the decision is made that for whatever reason the site is not appropriate for students at this time, call the office visited and thank them for their time. Be as diplomatic as possible as this will affect the program's PR image. Explain that there are no students interested in this particular area at this time, but their information will be kept in the program's listing of potential placements. Do not use a site unless it meets the program's and the school's standards.

SECTION THREE—DEVELOPING
THE INTERNSHIP LEARNING PLAN

Developing the Internship Learning Plan

The core of a quality internship program is some type of learning plan that describes a series of learning goals and the activities required to meet those goals. Students must complete the specified activities in order to fulfill the requirements of the internship program. With no curriculum or learning plan, internships often become nothing more than a journal and an attendance sheet. And students often end up performing low-level work that doesn't provide them the rich opportunities for learning that being out in the real world should.

When planning the goals and activities of an Internship Learning Plan, it is important to remember this is not the only course or activity in which the student is involved. They can't do everything, but they can certainly do a lot more than observe and listen. The important thing to remember is there must be goals and activities specific to this site—things that a student can only learn by being there and working alongside others. One of the overarching goals of any internship program is to help students gain the twenty-first-century skills that will be needed for the rest of their lives. There must be time for them to learn what's really important at the site, the things that can only be learned by doing.

Before moving on to the details of writing the learning plan, the role of students in planning the goals for their internships must be mentioned. Often, internship programs or internship components of larger projects, such as senior projects, require that students find their own internships and design their own learning plans. This does work for some students, but for many, asking students to write learning goals about a business or organization they know nothing about, for a job they haven't yet tried, in a field they haven't explored, is asking too much; it is a barrier to many and often results in vague goals that miss a great deal of the learning that could take place if a student had the guiding hand of an adult in setting those goals. For some students, even interviewing for an internship is a huge stretch. Getting to an internship should be a reach, but not a struggle. Students should have a hand in designing their learning, but they should not be expected to lay out a learning plan for an entire internship.

Essential Information in an Internship Learning Plan

In addition to writing the site-specific Internship Learning Plan, it helps to keep in mind that student interns will need direction in what learning activities are required of them and how to select suitable evaluation activities. A student handbook or seminar session to discuss this keeps the coordinator from having to repeat instructions over and over when students are placed.

Once the initial site visit is complete, the Internship Learning Plan needs to be written while the information is still fresh. Assemble all of the information gathered at the development visit and write the Intership Learning Plan for this site. Uniform goals (figure 2.3) are those goals that cross all career areas and can simplify the process of writing an Internship Learning Plan for each site. Some of the goals will work with certain placements and others will not. If some of the Uniform Goals are used, it is suggest that they be placed at the beginning of the Internship Learning Plan so that it will be easy to assign due dates for the selected goals.

Internship Learning Plans:

- should be specific to the site and should reflect what can actually take place at the unique site that's been developed.
- should answer the questions: "What can a student LEARN and DO at this site?"
- should be a collaboration between the Internship Coordinator and Internship Sponsor.
- should offer choices to students by allowing for revised and additional activities according to student need and interest.
- should contain reading and writing activities and activities that address workplace competencies.

Before writing site-specific goals, reviewing Uniform Goals and deciding which ones can be used for a particular internship site can save time.

Uniform Goals

		Due Date
☐	1. Journal	
☐	2. Literature in Field	
☐	3. Career Path Research	
☐	4. Vocabulary	
☐	5. Organization/Businesses Structure	
☐	6. Sponsor Interview	
☐	7. Entry for a Resume	
☐	8. Description for Transcript	
☐	9. Thank You Letter	
☐	10. Student Self Evaluation	
© 2007 *Internship Quest, LLC.* Reprinted courtesy of Internship Quest, LLC. *A Guide to Internship Program Development and Management*, 37. www.internshipquest.com		

Figure 2.3.   Uniform Goals

Uniform Goals

Uniform Goal 1: Journal

Practically every internship program requires students to keep some type of journal or log. This can be beneficial to the intern, or it can be a dreadfully boring list of mundane notations. Interns miss out on a great deal of reflective thinking if they aren't guided to pay attention to what is happening at the internship, think about their role in the activities, and to reflect on what it all means for them in their future. Rather than simply noting the date and what was accomplished, students need to be challenged to answer key questions such as: "Describe difficulties you are having in communication with someone at your site and how you resolved it or plan to resolve it." "Tell about a time you had to meet a deadline and how you went about doing that."

Uniform Goal 2: Literature in the Field

Every field has specific journals, trade magazines, and publications that are used for various purposes. The intern needs to become familiar with these sources of information from supply catalogs to professional peer-reviewed journals.

Uniform Goal 3: Career Path

One of the main goals for participating in an internship is to explore the area as a potential career path. Requiring the intern to actually learn what is required to become employed and successful in any field of endeavor is a key element of a successful internship experience. This is where the sponsor can be invaluable.

Uniform Goal 4: Vocabulary

Technical terms, special vocabulary, phrases, acronyms, and even jargon are found in practically all occupations. One way to help interns not shy away from asking what this specialized vocabulary means is to require that they show they know the meaning and usage of all terms and words.

Uniform Goal 5: Organization/Business Structure

It helps for interns to understand where they are in the structure of things. This might not be so important for someone interning at a two- or three-person business, but still, seeing the overall picture of who is in charge of what is something every intern should understand.

Uniform Goal 6: Sponsor Interview

This goal is one that can help the intern see not only the role career preparation and training played for the sponsor but how adults position themselves in the working world. It also helps the sponsor and intern get to know each other better. Many interns complete this goal early during the internship.

Uniform Goal 7: Entry for a Résumé

If interns do not complete this goal, they are missing an important aspect of doing an internship in the first place: getting real-world experience. They often need help condensing their internship experience into a résumé-size entry, but that is where the sponsor's or school's guidance comes in.

Uniform Goal 8: Description for a Transcript

A four-to-five-paragraph description that can be included on a student's transcript is important not only for the school to send to colleges and employers, but it helps the intern remember key aspects of the internship years later when they are asked to talk about their internship experience—and they often are asked. Returning students have reported that even five to seven years after they have completed an internship, prospective employers are still interested in what they did and what they feel they gained. As one student said, "I've gotten a lot of mileage out of that internship!"

Uniform Goal 9: Thank-You Letter

Internship coordinators would like to think that all of the young people in their programs know how important thank-you letters are. Alas, that is not always so. Therefore, requiring that a thank-you letter be sent to the sponsor for the time, guidance, and help provided is not unreasonable.

Uniform Goal 10: Student Self-Evaluation

At the end of the internship, the sponsor and the program coordinator will evaluate the student. Having a form for student self-evaluation adds to the entire internship experience and also provides feedback about a site to the program coordinator.

Evaluation Methods for Internship Learning Plan Activities

If possible, leave the decision about how to demonstrate internship site learning to the student. Have them select one or more of the activities/methods for demonstrating that each assigned activity has been completed and the goals of the internship have met. It is suggested that there be a variety of evaluation methods for each activity. Usually the program has some version of a student handbook or even a handout to explain how to select the appropriate evaluation activity and how to complete selected uniform goals.

Instead of having an intern write a report, an information brief—or a webcast, or a photo essay—might be more in keeping with what businesses actually use. Rather then explaining a process in writing, an intern can teach a class or small seminar or give a short presentation. With all of the technology students use today there is no reason why they must be tied to a potentially boring book or article reports. A key question when helping interns decide how to show what they know is "What is the practice at your placement for sharing information?"

Example of Possible Evaluation Methods for Internship Learning Plan Activities

Analyze in writing
Compare in writing
Complete a problem-
    solving project
Compose something
Conduct a survey

Conduct a trip or act as a
    guide at your internship
Create a brochure
Create a CD or DVD
    illustrating your
    work

Create a handbook
Create a work of art
Create and deliver
    a PowerPoint
    presentation or
    YouTube video

Debate with an opponent in person or in writing

Deliver an informative speech or lecture

Demonstrate or produce

Describe and define

Design sets and/or costumes

Evaluate results

Produce an event

Illustrate by graphs or charts

Produce a play

Produce a photo essay

Produce a podcast

Produce a video

Record a broadcast of a program

Research a topic and explain how it can be used in your internship

Teach a class

Write a business letter

Write memos

Write an ad

Write blog entries

The sample Internship Learning Plans in the appendix illustrate what such plans might look like, including the use of the Uniform Goals chart, which is a time-saving way to include these activities in all learning plans.

It is important to note that most students will not complete all of the goals and activities in a learning plan, and often, because of changes in the site activities or an intern's abilities or interests, goals will be added, removed, or revised. The Internship Learning Plan is best used as a starting point for the possible learning that can occur at a site, not as a rigid curriculum.

Getting It All Together

If records and forms can be kept in computer files and on a laptop, the program's organization will be simplified. However, there will undoubtedly still be a need for hard copies of most forms to take to sponsors and to site development visits. Students will also need to see copies of the Internship Learning Plan before committing to a particular internship.

After the site development process is complete, it is recommended that all pertinent forms, calendars, notifications, the program's version of a Memorandum of Agreement (example in the appendix), the district's liability agreement (examples in the appendix), and the Internship Learning Plan for the site be mailed or e-mailed to the sponsor for review.

The calendar for the semester or quarter is very important because businesses and organizations don't operate on the same schedules as schools. Sponsors are often puzzled when students suddenly don't show up the day after Thanksgiving or any other days that schools are closed.

When the paperwork related to this site is in place and the Internship Learning Plan is complete, it needs to be sent to the sponsor for review.

Once the sites are developed and all the paperwork is in place, the reward for all the upfront work begins—it is time to start placing students.

NOTE

1. John Dewey, *Experience and Education* (New York: Macmillan, 1938), 25.

Chapter Three

Placing Students in Internships

One Size Does Not Fit All

One size NEVER fits all. One size fits one. Period.

—Tom Peters[1]

This chapter covers the important role of the internship coordinator in placing students in the most appropriate internship site. It is up to the adults working with the internship program to steer students away from pursuing dead-end careers or selecting an internship simply because they happen to know someone in that career or have a relative there and have no idea what else might be available to them.

In addition, this chapter also discusses the importance of providing an orientation activity or booklet to prepare students for the internship experience, including preparing the student for the initial interview with the sponsor. The sponsor interview is a critical step in the internship process for all students. Even though the placements should not be competitive, the student needs to be aware right away that positions don't just happen and that an interview will be a part of work and real-life experiences from high school on. It is also key to the beginning of the sponsor/intern mentoring relationship.

INTERNSHIPS FOR ALL

As has been stated before, internships benefit *all* students and the importance of placing students in an internship site that is most likely to provide the best learning experience can't be stressed enough.

Matching the student with the best site to meet the student's interests is very important, but there are also other considerations to keep in mind. Some students will be quite easy to place, and, indeed, often find internship sites themselves. However, there are many students who need more guidance and support in locating and securing an internship site that will give them the best possible learning experience.

It is important for internship programs to be inclusive of *all* of the students the school serves. "Internship programs promote equity and reduce the experience gap by providing access to settings that are often closed to students from less privileged backgrounds."[2]

Sometimes, when internships are not mandatory, some students can be left out because of difficult application procedures, inexperience, ignorance of the opportunity in the first place, and belief that they will not qualify. Some students will need special help with the application process and securing an internship, and some will need additional help once placed. English language learners and students with disabilities often fall into this group.

It is the responsibility of the coordinator to discuss any special learning needs and adjustments interns may have and to help the sponsor plan how to address those needs. Informing those who will be working directly with an intern who will need learning accommodations will be helpful in the long run, keeping in mind the necessary regulations around student confidentiality.

Some interns may have special learning needs or language issues that require adjusting the way learning new skills are presented to them. Some may require written instructions in addition to verbal instructions along with demonstrations or they may require larger print documents. Interns still in the process of learning English may request that they not be required to speak in front of others at first, until they are comfortable with the language required of them. Or it may be necessary to place a student who is more accomplished in English, along with one who is not, in the same internship site.

But keeping in mind that no classroom can rival the practice of hearing, reading, writing, and speaking everyday English in a real-world setting, students have reported that their English language skills and confidence in using those skills have improved more rapidly through practice at an internship.

Research has demonstrated that work-based learning is one of the best ways to improve outcomes for youth with disabilities in secondary education.[3]

For the benefit of the internship program, consultation with colleagues in other departments is greatly encouraged. What better way is there to learn how to help a struggling student with a particular learning need than to consult her resource room teacher? Keeping the ELL and/or special education teacher involved with what his or her student is working on in the internship is not only a way to help the student but to build collegial support and relationships.

PLACING STUDENTS

Matching students to the proper site is key to a successful internship program. Many programs leave it up to students to locate and develop their own internship placements. Although this may work well for students who are self-assured or who have had experience with activities in the community away from the school campus, many students find the process of deciding on where they might look for an internship so daunting that they never even get as far as making the initial telephone call to set up an appointment for an interview.

The internship coordinator is the main liaison between the sponsor and the school and has the responsibility of finding a match between internship site and student. The coordinator knows if a sponsor is not likely to tolerate blue hair or body piercings. He or she knows if the student would fare best in a quiet, calm, organized atmosphere or if a livelier placement would be best.

While students are lining up their internship interviews, it is important to keep the sponsor in mind and in the loop. Even though there has been previous contact and all paperwork has been completed, the sponsor needs to know the program status, when to expect a potential intern to call, and when the internship is scheduled to begin. That way the sponsor can prepare the others on site for the arrival of an intern in the near future. It is also a good idea to remind the sponsor at this time of the importance of an official orientation.

Having a collection of sites that have been vetted by the internship coordinator or other adults connected with the school ensures having internship sites that are viewed as worthwhile and safe and sponsors who have been found to be reliable and interested in having an intern. In addition, the basic learning goals have been discussed with the sponsor and are in place, thus saving the program coordinator *and* the sponsor a great deal of time. Sponsors tend to step away from internship programs that make a huge demand on their time or expect them to develop student learning goals. This is not to say that students and sponsors should not have input into the goals and activities they will work on at the site, but schools have found that it is easier to change and fine-tune a learning plan than it is to create one from a blank page while other students are in line waiting for the coordinator's attention.

Hopefully students signing up for internships have had some lead-in preparation—but sometimes they have not. If this is the case, the internship coordinator will need to make sure students know what they are signing up for.

For those programs that do expect students to develop their own internship place-ments, it is useful to keep a record of sponsors so that future students who need help might be pointed in the right direction. The important thing is getting students out of the building and into the world of work with the guidance of responsible adults. The goal is student learning in the real world, not an obstacle course that will stymie student success.

Too often students have no idea where they might like to spend their internship time. They know of the "visible careers"—roles they see adults performing daily such as teachers, doctors, lawyers, sports stars, television personalities, public safety persons, and careers portrayed on television such as crime-scene investigators. But most young adults are not aware of the many careers that don't make the headlines of the papers such as health services support, scientific research, communications, tech-nology, social services, clerical work, behind-the-scenes retail work, office support, fieldwork—the list goes on.

Placing students is also dependent on what is realistically available in the com-munity. The student determined to become an actor will most likely not be able to intern with a national television series or Broadway production. However, the chance to work behind the scenes at a local theater might give him a very realistic picture of what needs to happen to produce the vehicle for "the star." Most students cannot intern with Google or Lucas Films, but many local communities have smaller companies that are involved with leading-edge technology and its application. And the student who is determined to be a professional athlete may need to begin their "career" under the supervision of an athletic trainer, physical therapist, or perhaps the district's athletic director.

Building Choice

As an internship program begins to grow and more and more students want to get out into the real world, it is important that the number and variety of sites also increase. Often a school may find it is easy to rely only on the specific connections they have in the community or on a few organizations that continue to offer internships rather than find new sites. The importance of having a variety of sites in a variety of organizations is that it gives students more opportunity to test out a career area that they may not know much about.

When looking for and adding new sites, the schools may want to review a framework of career clusters. The National Association of State Directors of Career Technical Education identifies sixteen career clusters that can be used as an organizing tool for curriculum design. And because the knowledge and skills required in these clusters encompass both secondary and postsecondary education, the framework informs efforts to strengthen and improve student transition from secondary to postsecondary education.[4]

A school may want to use their state's framework to ensure that the internship sites reflect more local career opportunities. The national or state framework is there as an organizing tool to help ensure that internship placements are available in all career clusters. An example of how a school can use the national framework to categorize potential internship sites can be seen in figure 3.1.

Framework: Career Clusters and Internships

When using any framework it is important to think about and identify what an intern can learn in any particular career cluster. This can help the teacher guide a student to a site where he or she can apply specific knowledge and learn additional skills. The framework can also enable the student to see potential career areas that he might not have otherwise considered.

The process of using a framework as an organizing tool allows the teacher or internship coordinator to think "outside the box" when discussing possible placements with students. Some new ideas that the framework can provide are:

- Turn part-time work into an internship site. Many students want or need to work while still in school and many of those jobs held by students could easily be dismissed as not being ideal internship sites. Working in a fast-food restaurant or at the local gas station may not be high on the list of internship opportunities a school may want to have for its students and yet these sites can be a good learning opportunity if the teacher asks, "What can a student learn there?" There is much to

Framework: Career Clusters and Internships

Cluster	What Can an Intern Learn	Areas of Placement
Agriculture, Food & Natural Resources	Interns can apply their knowledge in science as they learn more about protecting the natural environment, harvest natural resources and raise animals	*Florist, nursery, landscaping, veterinarian practice, conservation, farm*
Architecture & Construction	Interns can apply their math skills and learn about designing, planning, managing and building	*Architectural firm, construction material company, home building company, local government planning*
Arts, A/V Technology & Communications	Interns can apply their skills in writing, performing and designing. They can further build their skills in communication.	*Artisans, graphic arts, multi-media production (radio and television), local theaters, local newspaper*
Business Management & Administration	Interns will be a supporting role for all business and management activities. They will have opportunities to learn planning and organizing skills as well as problem solving.	*Local business or non-profit with administration departments*
Education & Training	Interns will assist in providing educational services. They will gain an understanding of how individuals learn and further build their communication skills.	*Teaching assistant, pre-school assistant, educational support staff assistant, sports program*
Finance	Interns can apply their skills in math. They will learn about the various activities in the finance sectors. They can build their problem-solving skills.	*Banking customer services, local accounting practice, local insurance company or agency*
Government & Public Administration	Interns will support government at all levels and learn about the interactions between government and the people. They can apply their knowledge of history, civics, and political science.	*Local town office departments, non-profit organizations working with government*
Health Science	Interns can apply their knowledge in science and also build interpersonal skills when working with clients and patients. The can further build their team working skills.	*Local dental, doctor offices, local hospital departments, physical therapy practice, local health clinics*
Hospitality & Tourism	Interns will learn about the service industry and build customer service skills. They can further build their communication and team working skills.	*Local hotel, local tourism office, conference centers, restaurants, catering companies*

Figure 3.1.   Career Framework

Cluster	What Can an Intern Learn	Areas of Placement
Human Services	Interns can add value to their community in providing assistance to individuals and families. They can build interpersonal skills through client management and providing services.	*Social work agency, senior centers, local food bank*
Information Technology	Interns can apply their knowledge in computer science. The will learn about systems integration, new media, hardware, and software. They can learn and apply problem-solving skills.	*Local computer companies, businesses with IT departments, local government IT*
Law, Public Safety, Corrections & Security	Interns can add value to their community by assisting and supporting criminal justice system, legal and protective services. They can build good communication and client services skills.	*Local law offices, EMS, Fire Department, Sherriff's department, local court services*
Manufacturing	Interns can apply science and math knowledge in the production and processing of products. They can learn planning and organizing skills as well as problem solving.	*Local manufacturing company*
Retail/Wholesale Sales and Services	Interns can apply their communication skills and learn sales techniques. They can learn planning and organizing skills.	*Local store, business to business sales organization*
Marketing	Interns can apply their math skills as they assist in market research. They can learn how sales and marketing are related and learn planning and organizing skills and problem-solving skills.	*Local advertising agency, public relations agency, market research company, business with marketing department*
Science, Technology, Engineering & Mathematics	Interns can apply their science and math skills. They will learn how these skills are used in lab settings, testing services, and research and development.	*Local engineering company, local medical lab, business with research and development, renewable energy companies and non-profits*
Transportation, Distribution & Logistics	Interns can learn the logistics of transportation and apply science and math. They will learn planning and organizing and problem-solving skills.	*Local airport, automotive service, local warehouse distribution center, bicycle repair shop, district school bus provider*
Adapted from "The 16 Career Clusters®," National Association of State Directors of Career Technical Education Consortium, Career Clusters.		

Figure 3.1. (*continued*)

learn about franchising and logistics of planning in a fast-food restaurant, and a gas station, a student can investigate the economics of the highs and lows of gas prices, for example. If the work the student does at a part-time job is separate in time and activities, then an internship experience is possible.

- Local government is not only the mayor's office. Local government can offer a variety of learning opportunities not only in politics and civics, but also in areas such as how services are delivered and how town water is tested for microbes. Students don't have to be interested in politics to take a placement in government.
- Manufacturing is not just an assembly line. Local manufacturing companies have a variety of jobs from production to quality control, product testing, warehousing, transportation logistics, and coordinating sales forecast with product production.
- Internships are a way for students to test out different careers. What a student learns in one career area can easily be applied to another. For example, a student who takes an internship on a farm may start to learn about the marketing of the farm's products and this could spark an interest in marketing in general and take her in a new career direction.

> *Just because you have an internship there doesn't mean you will work there. —Internship Coordinator.*

- Non-profits are businesses too. Non-profits face many of the challenges of for-profit companies. Whether placed in a non-profit or for-profit company, students can learn about accounting, customer service, how to write a business plan, and how to achieve specified goals. Students interested in business find that there is much to learn in non-profits.

Whatever framework, state or national, is used, it is only a tool that gives the teacher/coordinator some new ways of looking at and finding potential internship sites.

Dreaming Big

I run on the road, long before I dance under the lights.[5]

—Muhammad Ali, American boxer

Sometimes students have a very clear idea of what they want to do. It is not uncommon to hear "I want to be a sports star." Or "I want to be a recording/TV/movie star." Or sometimes students want to find an internship in a field that they have seen on TV such as crime-scene investigation, or they may see themselves as the next app developer. These students should not be discouraged but they need to know the steps they will need to take in order to achieve their dream.

There are two steps a teacher or coordinator can take to help these students gain a realistic understanding about what they need to do in the here and now as they start on their way. First, gain an awareness of what the local community college has to offer. Today many community colleges offer study in new and exciting areas. Some offer programs in sports management, app development, forensic science, computer animation, screenwriting, and music marketing. Helping students to be aware of what is available after graduation makes them more realistic about the steps they need to take to achieve their dream.

Second, for community college and high school students who are interested in an exciting career, finding an internship in their area of interest can help them see what other careers may be available for them. Using a career framework can help the teacher/coordinator think widely about where some of these jobs may exist and where a student can find an internship.

A student focused on a career in crime-scene investigation could find real work experience in forensics in a hospital, medical examiner's office, or state and local law enforcement. A student who has her heart set on using her computer skills as a game designer, app developer, or security/internet expert could find interesting opportunities in advertising agencies, architectural firms, local TV, graphic design companies, or educational publishing. There may not be a sports management company nearby but an internship at a fitness club, sports recreation department, or with a local sports team can be the start to a career.

Many young people have a dream. And an internship that is well chosen and appropriate can help them start on a road to achieving that dream or help understand the reality of work in that field.

Keeping Track of Internship Sites

Most programs, no matter the size, list the internships that they have developed in some type of database. This can range from a simple list with a brief description and contact information to a commercially printed catalog of available sites stored in a sophisticated, searchable database. This can serve to help students think beyond their existing views of the work people do.

Ideally, students should have a choice of placements. Although some students have remarked that any internship is better than no internship during their senior year, most would agree that a meaningful internship is better than just any placement. Newer programs may not have the luxury of multiple placements in every interesting career area. Some programs will never offer that luxury but if a student is interested in science, every effort should be made to match him with a science placement and not try to make do with a cultural arts center.

Some students have no idea what an internship is about, even if they have read the description or seen the Internship Learning Plan. Often it is the coordinator's job to explain to them what they can expect, and at other times this preparation takes place in a class. No matter where it takes place, every student needs help preparing for the initial interview and an orientation to internships in general.

STUDENTS AND THE SPONSOR INTERVIEW

The interview with the sponsor is often very difficult for a student. Going to a new, unfamiliar place, or speaking with an unknown adult is not easy for most students, many of whom have had little interviewing experience. That is why many do not schedule or show up for the interview. For some students, a handout that explains how to set up an interview is all they need. Other students may need extra support for this. Sometimes this step is enough to stop a student cold. They practically need a script and the teacher sitting beside them while they make the phone call. And that is fine. Hopefully by the end of the internship, they will have more confidence.

Students need three documents for their interviews:

- A one-pager on how to succeed at an interview. This may be the first interview a student has been on and they have no idea what to expect. If they can role-play in a class, great, but some students don't have that opportunity. Some hints about what to expect and how to handle some of the basics of interviewing, like handshakes, gum, attire, eye contact can help them through what can be a nerve-wracking experience.
- A letter of introduction from the school, which should have a space for the sponsor's name, address, and telephone number.
- An application and/or résumé. As much as we would like students to be able to produce a professional résumé, we forget that many students haven't really done much of anything and their résumés are pretty sparse. One of the reasons they are participating in an internship is to be able to learn about a career area and to be able to put that experience on a résumé. Sometimes an application is more informative to a prospective sponsor.

One important thing to remember is that the interview process should not be competitive. An internship is not a contest. Students should not be forced to compete for placements. Internships at the high school and community college level should be designed to support the students while they are under the protective guidance of adults who know them. They are stepping out into the real world but they still need a guiding hand.

The interview should be an opportunity for both parties to get acquainted, and for the student's responsibilities to be discussed. This is the time for the student and sponsor to talk about why the student wants to intern at this site and for the student to learn a bit more about the site than might have been presented in a listing of internships. They can talk about what some of the tasks might be during the internship and the sponsor can get to know a bit about the student's interests and activities.

If either the student or sponsor feels that the "fit" isn't right, they should feel free to say so. A program works best when both student and sponsor have freedom to make choices about things that affect them both. If the sponsor turns down the student, make sure the reason is clear. Perhaps the student felt the interview went well. If that is the case, you will have to explain the problem to the student carefully, being mindful of their self-esteem. This is all part of a learning experience. If it's the student who says no, make sure it's not just nervousness speaking.

Sponsors that turn down many students should be removed from the list of available internships. Internship learning is about educating students. If a sponsor consistently does not accept your students, or is too selective, the program needs a different sponsor.

ORIENTATION TO INTERNSHIPS

Once students have completed the interview process and the correct match is made, it is time for some type of orientation. If this important step is missed, the school and the students will not reap all of the benefits of the internship experience.

The students have questions. The school and internship site have standards and expectations. The best way to communicate this is through group meetings, classes, or orientation sessions although this might not always be possible. At the very least, a student orientation handbook or handout should be available for each intern.

What Should an Orientation to Internship Include?

A student's orientation to what to expect at an internship experience should include:

- *Explanation of the intern's primary responsibility*
  The intern needs to understand, even before beginning the internship experience, that the main responsibility at the site is twofold—completing the goals of the Internship Learning Plan and discussing tasks with the sponsor.

  Sometimes a student needs to be reminded that the goal of the internship is to learn and that completing the goals and activities of the Internship Learning Plan helps them to achieve that goal. It is easy to forget that the student is not an employee but a learner, and to gain the most from this experience the intern will need the flexible structure of the Internship Learning Plan. It will provide guidance during those times when the sponsor is not readily available for direction or to assign a project or task.

  The intern also needs to know that, in addition to the Internship Learning Plan, the sponsor will have additional tasks and assignments and the intern is expected to complete those to the best of her ability. Workflow in the real world is not predictable and interns need to be reminded that more than likely a plan that has been made or task assigned may change based on the needs of the internship site and that flexibility shows maturity.
- *Being aware of and understanding attendance policy and school closure days*
  The intern needs to be reminded of the school's policy on attendance and that attending the internship placement is equal to attending class. Some programs specify that no absences are excused and that if a student cannot attend the internship, the time needs to be made up, as in the real world. The schools that have this type of policy should make arrangements with sponsors to have students make up missed time on days other than their regularly scheduled times, or on weekends or school holidays.

  The student will have to make the decision whether or not to attend the internship on days when the school is officially closed. However, experience has shown that most interns are very happy to report to their internships, even during extended school vacations, and the sponsors are happy to have them. All interns need to know that the accepted way to deal with lateness or absence from a work site is to call the sponsor *early*, preferably a day or so ahead, *and* to inform the school of the absence.

• *Time schedule, safety, and behavior policies*

This aspect of the internship should be covered during the sponsor's orientation of the students but it is helpful to remind students that they are responsible for knowing the placement's safety and behavior policies and procedures.

• *Proper attire and personal grooming requirements for an internship placement*

Some students feel they must wear adult business attire for their internships and are very concerned that they don't have suits and jackets, and some feel that after-school casual dress is just fine. Schools need to help interns assess what is proper attire for their particular placements. Reminding students to ask about attire during the interview is one way of dealing with this issue. Students are much more likely to take direction about attire from the sponsor, but often the responsibility for making sure students are not calling negative attention to themselves in their dress, or are so concerned about having the proper clothing that they miss the benefits of the internship experience, falls to the internship coordinator. Often, a coordinator, teacher, or previous intern can be helpful in talking with students about the issues of excessive jewelry, perfume and aftershave, hair, and appropriate footwear.

It is surprising to many adults that some students simply don't know that T-shirts with offensive language, ripped jeans, shorts, tank tops, sweat pants, and wearing hats indoors are not appropriate for the world of work. Simply suggesting collared shirts and clean slacks for boys, and blouses or sweaters and skirts or slacks for girls, are sometimes all it takes to head off potential problems.

• *Being aware of and understanding the site's policies in regard to computer and other office equipment and supplies*

Again, the sponsor should cover this during orientation on the site, but in general students need to be reminded that businesses have policies about how their resources are to be used and the intern is responsible for learning these policies. Some interns have no idea that there are such people as supply secretaries and that this is where they get the supplies they need. (It is never too early for an intern to learn the importance of making this person their friend.) If a student is assigned a computer station, the correct use of it for business purposes is something to be stressed. Although interns are not in placements to serve as copy-room experts, they do need to learn how to correctly use the copy machine, and the smart intern quickly learns who is in charge of this and seeks out direction before having an unfortunate experience with one of today's complicated machines.

• *Use of cell phones during business hours*

Both the school and the sponsor need to address this issue, and probably several times. Interns need to be made very aware of when they may use their own cell phones while at their placements, and the school can help them see that using a cell phone for personal use is taking time away from responsibilities at the internship site. Texting during meetings is also another problem area. Interns often see employees doing this and feel that the behavior is acceptable. Frequent reminders by the coordinator and sponsor need to stress that this is not acceptable and the best practice is to lock the phone away for the duration of the internship time.

• *Confidentiality issues*

Many placements deal with information that is confidential or proprietary, and the sponsor will need to inform the intern during the orientation what their policy is in this regard and how important it is to be professional about this very important matter. This is also a good topic of discussion for a seminar or group meeting, as many interns will encounter this issue in their placements and future employment.

• *Use of social networking sites*

As students are preparing to enter the world of work or further education, the adults around them often wonder if they are aware of the numerous articles about the effect (usually negative) social networking sites have on a person's ability to find employment or get accepted into an educational institution. Seminars or classes to support internships and mentoring sessions with sponsors are perfect opportunities to address the issue of the effects social networking profiles have, and will continue to have, on students as they move into the adult world.

• *Attending seminars and mentoring sessions*

Interns need to know their schedules for seminars and mentoring sessions in addition to the days scheduled for the internship. If the school has regular times for these group meetings, they need to be part of the student's official schedule and the intern should know that attendance is not optional.

• *Knowing different ways to get to the internship site*

Rare is the adult who has not encountered difficulties getting to work for one reason or another. Students don't often think about this issue when planning how to get to their internship sites. Time spent with Google Maps or MapQuest, a paper map, a GPS app on a student's phone, or just discussing various ways to get from either the student's home or school to the internship site helps the student see that planning ahead is something that working adults do. Usually this is a good topic for a pre-internship group meeting as students often have many more solutions than the adults involved.

• *Completing the end-of-internship evaluation*

Interns should keep in mind throughout their internship that at the end they will be completing an evaluation of the entire experience—and that this is to serve as part of their self-evaluation and will serve to give feedback to the school about the activities provided by the internship site. Therefore, they should be encouraged to keep notes during their internship experience so that the evaluation can reflect their progress over time.

Once the student's interview has taken place, the orientation has been completed, and all paperwork is in place, it's time for the intern to step out into the real world.

NOTES

1. Tom Peters, *Leadership* (Essentials Series, DK Publishing) (New York: DK Publishing, 2005), 139. Used by permission of Tom Peters. See www.tompeters.com for further information.

2. Eliot Levine, "The Rigors and Rewards of Internships," *Educational Leadership* 68, no. 1 (September 2010): 46.

3. Thomas R. Bailey, Katherine L. Hughes, and David Thornton Moore, *Working Knowledge: Work-based Learning and Education Reform* (New York: Routledge, 2004), 3.

4. National Association of State Directors of Carerr Technical Education Consortium. "The 16 Career Clusters®." Accessed May 15, 2013. http://careertech.org/careerclusters/glance/clusters-occupations.html.

5. Muhammad Ali, as quoted in David Hazlehurst, "Chapter 15: Designing Stories," in *Changing the Fourth Estate: Essays on South African Journalism* (Cape Town, South Africa: HSRC Press, 2005), 154.

Chapter Four

Monitoring Students in Internships
Providing a Guiding Hand

> Monitoring, by whatever means, will be most effective when it is built into the plan for the internship.
>
> —Robert P. Inkster and Roseanna Gaye Ross[1]

This chapter focuses on the details of monitoring students throughout the internship experience. Although internships are one way students can gain real-world experience and learn skills critical for the next stage of their lives, it can't be assumed that students are getting the most out of an internship merely by being there. In addition to keeping the internship on track, active monitoring shows the student and sponsor that the school is an active participant in the internship experience. Underlying the importance of monitoring students on site is the element of relationships, the foundation on which truly meaningful internships are built.

MONITORING STUDENTS IN INTERNSHIPS

Monitoring the student's progress during an internship experience is an important key to a successful internship. This activity helps build the three-way relationship between the school, the sponsor, and the student. It allows the coordinator to know what is going on at the placement, ensures that learning is occurring, and helps to head off any problems early on. Monitoring also allows the coordinator to establish a relationship with the sponsor and build a continuous connection between the sponsor and the school.

It is through the monitoring of internship sites that the school can ensure that the internship experience is genuinely educative.

Monitoring internship experiences is much more than having a student hand in an attendance sheet and a journal on the last day. We owe it to students to help them get the most out of the internship experience by guiding their learning and reflection throughout to ensure they are gaining the skills needed for the future. Unmonitored internships can often devolve into a series of boring, repetitive tasks from which the student gains nothing.

Often workers in a site are more than happy to dump unwanted tasks on the intern, and at first, doing the "grunt" work in an office or placement might help the student learn some of the necessary, boring skills everyone does in the workplace. But if only "grunt work" fills the intern's day, something needs to change. And usually the intern needs help from the school in effecting that change. Without close monitoring by the school, it may be weeks before it is discovered that interns are not doing the work they are supposed to be doing. Perhaps the sponsor is new and feels that giving the intern more challenging work might rock the boat as the intern seems quite happy doing the work he is involved with.

Many students are not keen on reporting that things are not going as they should be, fearing that they may cause problems for the sponsor or even may be removed from the internship site. And some interns, having no previous experience in the world of work, assume "grunt work" is all they are going to be permitted to do. The novelty of being in the real world hasn't yet worn off and they are quite content to make copies, get coffee, and serve as a general "gofer." Often the solution is just a matter of the coordinator intervening to re-center the focus of the internship, reviewing the learning plan's goals and activities, supporting the sponsor in assigning tasks, and reviewing expectations with both the sponsor and intern, and things soon get back on track.

It is important to note that monitoring is not checking up. Dropping in unexpectedly to visit a student is not respectful of the student's or sponsor's time. Making an appointment helps the intern learn that this is how people in the business world conduct business, manage their time, and respect others' time. Of course, if the intern is involved in a special activity such as leading part of a project, making a presentation, or interacting with customers and clients, that would be the best time to schedule a visit.

Importance of Internship Relationships

Rita Pierson, a teacher, in a recent TED Talk, stated, "One of the things we rarely discuss [in education] is the value and importance of human connections—relationships."[2]

This statement goes to the core of a quality internship: relationships with adults in the real world. The coordinator is essential in building the relationship between herself and the sponsor and the student by being available and on-site as often as possible. The coordinator also encourages the growth of the relationship between the sponsor and intern.

In a quality internship program, an internship coordinator's primary responsibilities ideally should be external to the school building. She should have a schedule permitting as much time in the field as possible. To ensure the program's success—especially during a pilot program, when everything is new and the program is facing all the problems of a start-up—consideration should be given to scheduling as much time for field visits and telephone follow-ups as possible. This is critical to building the important relationships that are the foundation of quality internships. If monitoring is built in to the schedule, then it will not become an afterthought.

Unfortunately, the ideal is not always possible, and many internship programs are forced to operate mainly with telephone and e-mail communications. Although that is not ideal, it is better than sending students to the field at the beginning of the semester and never speaking to or communicating with the sponsor throughout the duration of the internship. Some schools come to a compromise and find a way to release coordinators to visit only new, potential sponsor sites or those that seem to be having difficulties with the intern. Other schools arrange limited released time for coordinators to visit sites once a year during specific "down" times in the school. At the very least, each sponsor and intern should have access to the coordinator via telephone and e-mail.

GUIDELINES FOR MONITORING STUDENT PERFORMANCE

Site Visits

In the ideal internship world, a site visit might be conducted two or more times during a quarter or semester. In reality this probably does not happen that often. However, when there is time for a site visit it is important to get the most out of it.

The purpose of the site visit is:

- to create and nurture a relationship with the student
- to create and nurture a relationship with the sponsor
- to observe and evaluate student performance
- to observe and evaluate the performance of the sponsor
- to demonstrate to both student and sponsor that the school is indeed interested in the learning outcomes as stated in the initial agreement

Primarily, a site visit is a chance for the student and coordinator to deal with each other on a one-to-one basis. Perhaps during the orientation and placement process, the intern was just one of many students interacting with the coordinator. During a visit, there is less likelihood of interruptions and distractions. The coordinator from the school is a familiar adult, and in the setting of the workplace, the relationship between her and the student is more than that of teacher to student. The visit provides the intern with another opportunity to interact with an adult in the real world, not just the school setting. The sponsor has been working as a mentor/teacher in a one-on-one relationship throughout the internship, providing the intern with more time with a caring adult. Perhaps other adults in the workplace have also been interacting and developing relationships with the intern. All of these new adult relationships serve to introduce the intern to what he can expect in the years after graduation.

Visiting on-site also provides a direct feedback loop to view the performance of the sponsor. Viewing performance does not mean judging. It means observing and seeing how the sponsor interacts with the intern. Is the student treated differently from other staff? What kind of desk or other work site does the student have? Is the student being treated with just the right kind of exacting standards and understanding? By visiting on a regular basis, everyone concerned sees that the school is indeed interested and that the representative from the school, because of experience with many other interns, has a wealth of knowledge to share when it comes to day-to-day dealing with interns.

If, because of scheduling or a large number of interns, regular site visits are not possible, at least a phone call should be made to the sponsor to check on the intern's progress. Schools and sponsors comfortable with technology may be able to effect an electronic site visit via Skype or another face-to-face program, but there is really nothing comparable to meeting student and sponsor in person and nurturing the connection and relationship that is so important in a successful internship experience. The key is nurturing the relationship with the sponsor and the student and keeping the lines of communication open. "Relationships are the medium of the internship experience; they are the context in which most of (the) learning and growth occurs."[3]

Structure and Purpose of the Internship Site Visit

Each site visit (or telephone/Skype contact) should serve as a test of the continued effectiveness of the internship and serves to assure that:

- the Internship Learning Plan is being fulfilled;
- the student's interest is high and the student is learning;
- there is consistent quality supervision;
- the sponsor knows that the school has not just sent a student out to fend for himself.

The internship visit has four components:

- Observing student performance
- Private discussion with student
- Private discussion with sponsor
- Three-way discussion: student/internship coordinator/sponsor

Observing student performance and "private time" with the student is key to a visit. Time or scheduling constraints may not always permit observation of the intern interacting with clients or other staff, processing paperwork, or performing other hands-on tasks, but it's a good idea to visit then if possible. If the student is acting in a theater company or escorting tours through a museum, try to make the time to be there.

A private discussion with the student is an opportunity for several outcomes:

- Clarification of Internship Learning Plan activities and outcomes.
- Seeing if the student is accomplishing the goals and activities laid out at the beginning of the internship? Are they too difficult or too easy? Has the student's assignment changed, requiring a revision of Internship Learning Plan assignments? If so, a change of goals on the spot may be required.
- Review of the student's log or journal.
- Discussion of personal and maturity problems that interfere with work at this internship or in other matters.
- Determining if the student perceives the sponsor as uninterested or unfair? Does the student want new assignments but does not know how to ask? The coordinator

may be able to problem solve with the intern, or he might feel that a referral to the guidance department would be useful.

A private meeting with the sponsor also has several objectives:

- It allows the sponsor and coordinator to evaluate the student's performance and begin to plan steps to enhance the education process. It is also a time to evaluate the sponsor's performance.
- Sponsors sometimes need to be reminded that their student-interns are indeed students, and not unpaid labor. The bottom line for this process is the achievement of learning outcomes. Ask which learning objectives have already been reached and which remain.
- Some sponsors are better teachers than the educators who are paid to teach, but others are not. Some are better supervisors and mentors as well. No matter what the case, many have little time or skill in handling students who are not mature or highly motivated. Such consultations can help the sponsor through a problem with the student as much as helping the student with any problems, real or perceived, with the sponsor.

The three-way discussion is crucial. In this meeting:

- Discuss where the education process is headed, how to achieve the goals laid out in the Internship Learning Plan, and also address any problems that may have come up.
- Get added responsibility for the student, or scale it back, based on the assessment of the intern's performance.
- Address problems the student has mentioned in private, if the student gives permission. The coordinator can act as the student's representative, but, even better, the coordinator can use his or her presence to support and empower the student to voice his or her own concerns, thus learning how to solve problems rather than avoiding them.

The coordinator needs to keep the warning signs of potential problems in mind during all visits and calls. Sometimes signs are really just the result of frustration and misunderstanding and can be rectified easily. At other times, signs of problems signify that issues need to be addressed immediately. It is difficult to tell the severity of the signs without observing and assessing in person, hence, the recommendation that field visits be built into the framework of the internship program from the beginning.

Warning Signs of Potential Internship Problems

- Conflicts between sponsor and intern
- Conflicts with other workers
- Too much grunt work
- Student disengagement
- Student's personal problems
- Too much/too little meaningful work

EVALUATING THE INTERNSHIP LEARNING PLAN

Final evaluation of the Internship Learning Plan takes place at the end of the internship period, which does not mean that evaluation is not taking place throughout. Because this is an important aspect of quality internship programs, all of chapter 7 is devoted to this topic.

All along, the coordinator has been checking intermediate assignments, examining and helping with preparations for larger-scale assignments, and observing on-task performance. For performance-based outcomes—from shoeing a horse to acting with a theater group—the coordinator has personally witnessed the student in action. When visits weren't possible, the school, sponsor, and student have kept in touch by phone or e-mail.

The sponsor, who has been ensuring that the student fulfills requirements, is almost an equal partner in this. He or she has been checking assignments prior to the student giving them to the coordinator. He or she should review all final reports. Who is better able to evaluate the subject-area content of the chemistry lab reports, glossary definitions, computer-aided-design drawings, weight-training regimens, or other technical matters in which the student has received training?

The student needs to know the deadline for handing in the end-of-internship work. Some schools allow a certain number of days of leeway, after which credit cannot be made up. The final evaluation is in the school's hands, not the sponsor's. The center of any internship program always remains with the school. In most cases, both parties are in agreement. They know what the student has or has not accomplished. But as the educator, charting the student's path through school with guidance counselors and other school staff, the school must have the final word in granting or not granting credit if credit is to be given for the internship.

In summary, it is the role of the internship coordinator to be the connection between the student, sponsor, and school. He or she is responsible for overseeing the successes and troubleshooting the problems at all internship sites.

NOTES

    1. Robert P. Inkster and Roseanna Gaye Ross, *The Internship as Partnership: A Handbook for Campus-based Coordinators and Advisors* (Raleigh, NC: National Society for Experiential Education, 1995), 65.

    2. Rita Pierson, "Every Kid Needs a Champion," TED | Talks | Education, May 2013. www.ted.com/talks/rita_pierson_every_kid_needs_a_champion.

    3. H. Frederick Sweitzer and Mary A. King, *The Successful Internship: Personal, Professional, and Civic Development* (Belmont, CA: Brooks/Cole, 2009), 8.

Chapter Five

Supporting Sponsors in Internships

Building a Strong Partnership

Every intern has a supervisor, but only some get a mentor.

—Thomas R. Bailey[1]

This chapter discusses the importance of supporting the sponsor during the intern's time on site and talks about ways the school, through the internship coordinator, can offer the sponsor guidance, ideas, and suggestions, to ensure that the internship experience is a positive one for all concerned and that the sponsor does not feel over-whelmed by the responsibility of having an intern.

THE IMPORTANCE OF RELATIONSHIPS

As mentioned in the previous chapter, the key to good internships is good relation-ships. And one of the keys to a good three-way relationship among the sponsor, stu-dent, and school is support of the sponsor. One of the first things potential sponsors remark is that they aren't teachers. It is important to stress that they aren't expected to be "teachers" in the traditional way but rather mentors/guides. The main difference between being a teacher in a classroom and a mentor in a workplace is the one-to-one relationship. Sponsors also need to know that in addition to serving as a mentor they will also be fulfilling the role of supervisor, something they most likely do on a daily basis.

It is helpful for sponsors to know that their role as a mentor is invaluable and that research has shown that "the two factors which are the best predictors of personal growth [of interns] are opportunities to act autonomously and to develop collegial relationships with adults."[2] And it is in the collegial, mentoring relationship that real-world learning occurs.

PREPARING THE SPONSOR FOR THE INTERNSHIP

Before any discussion of support of a sponsor, preparation of the sponsor needs to be mentioned. Too often businesses and organizations sign up for an intern and really have no clear idea as to what the program entails. Some think they are getting extra workers. Some think they must spend the entire time alongside the intern. It is incumbent on the school to make sure sponsors know what they are getting into and what is expected of them. To save time, many programs produce or purchase a sponsor handbook so that sponsors have the information they will need before the intern arrives. Whether the information is imparted personally by the coordinator, in a group orientation held at the school or business, or through a booklet, there are several important things a sponsor needs to know before the internship begins.

What Sponsors Need to Know (before the intern arrives)

The School's Definition of an Internship

Before the sponsors sign on to provide a work-based learning experience for a student, it is important that they understand what the school defines as an internship. An internship can be defined as any carefully monitored and structured work experience in which a student has intentional learning goals and reflects on what he or she is learning throughout the experience. Each school will have its own unique definition, but most definitions include some of the basic characteristics of a quality internship, which include:

- A work-based learning experience of about three to six months (a quarter or semester)
- Is generally a one-time experience
- May be full- or part-time
- May be paid or nonpaid
- May be evaluated for academic credit
- Has structured learning objectives
- Has learning activities include goals, observation, demonstration, evaluation, and assessment
- Is a balance between the intern's learning goals and the specific work of the organization
- Aims for academic, career, and personal development

What Is Expected of the Sponsor during the Internship?

Sponsors need to be informed ahead of time that interns will come to their organization or business to learn about the world of work. They will not be regular employees and will need the sponsor's time, guidance, mentoring, and coaching. As they begin to learn new skills and behaviors, they will be able to add value to the organization. The sponsor will also need to be reminded that he will be serving in two roles—the role of supervisor and the role of mentor.

In the supervisory role, the sponsor will delegate tasks and responsibilities to their interns, choosing to focus on the task at hand. As a mentor the sponsor will guide the intern on the skills they need to get ahead, academically and professionally. They will lay out expectations and guidelines and still give the student room to think creatively, thus helping the intern map out career pathways and learn how to network to get that next internship or first job or select a program of education. It is in this role as mentor that the importance of building a solid relationship comes into play. "The best mentoring relationships occur spontaneously between supervisors and interns. The effective mentor makes sure that the intern becomes part of the organization very quickly and is given highly visible tasks. This type of mentor ensures that the intern is introduced to the professionals through such resources as networking, luncheons, and conferences."[3]

Sponsors are used to being supervisors but often they need support in the role of mentor, and the coordinator or site developer can stress that the one-on-one relationship and time spent together are the basis of a quality mentoring experience.

What Is in It for the Sponsor?

In addition to explaining what is expected of the sponsor, it is also a good idea to explain how sponsors and their companies or organizations are benefited by internships.

Internships benefit sponsors by:

- Providing the organization with a year-round source of highly motivated pre-professionals
- Bringing new perspectives to old problems
- Training as candidates for temporary or seasonal positions and projects in the future
- Providing opportunity for organizations to train potential employees in the most up-to-date technologies
- Enabling the organization or company to contribute to the next generation's preparation for the real world
- Enhancing the organization's image in the community

What Young People Are Like?

All sponsors need to be reminded that adolescence can be a turbulent time during which young people struggle to define their personality and find their place in the world. Late adolescence is a time when young people begin to define their sense of self and test their ideas in the adult world. While it is sometimes a challenge to work with adolescents, it is also very exciting and rewarding to be part of this period of rapid learning and personal growth.

The sponsor may want to know that "the most intensive forms of workplace learning—apprenticeship and sustained internships—are especially effective in meeting the developmental needs of young people. They provide a structure to support the transition from adolescence to adulthood lacking for the majority of young people in the U.S."[4] And the sponsor can be a part of helping a young person during this transition.

Although adolescents involved in work-based learning can demonstrate their ability to take on adult responsibilities successfully and meet real-world expectations, they also face many personal challenges in their journey to adulthood. This is a time of burgeoning independence during which the adolescent shows he is:

- eager for opportunities to make decisions—yet is often insecure about the process of making these decisions;
- uneasy about his preparation for the future—sometimes evidenced by avoidance and exhibiting an attitude of complacence;
- sometimes apt to challenge authority—and not very politely either. Adolescents have not yet learned how to question without hostility in many situations, nor have they learned how to accept constuctive criticism. Too often, criticism is viewed as an attack on them personally;
- very interested in physical appearance—his own standard, not an adult's. Adolescent appearance can often be misinterpreted by adults as a form of rebellion or need to "belong" but most interns will quickly see what the standard is in the workplace and usually adjust their appearance accordingly, showing willingness to "belong" to a different peer group on the days of their internships;
- eager to try out different values and build his own philosophies—and these can be a source of meaningful mentoring discussions;
- desirous of respect from adults—although he may feign indifference;
- eager for independence and privileges but he may have trouble with responsibility and personal discipline;
- feeling a sense insecurity in new settings with adults, even though he puts on an air of confidence.

How to Help the Intern Learn

Although sponsors often feel they are not "teachers" in the usual sense of the word, they actually teach all the time. As supervisors and team members and leaders in their own work situations, they are sharing information and know-how with colleagues daily. When this is pointed out to them, they become more comfortable with the role of mentor and supervisor to an intern.

It helps to provide sponsors with a list of the basic steps to take when working with an intern on new tasks. Interns want to learn new skills and often learn best with hands-on practice. This five-step learning outline will ensure successful learning with the intern:

- Ask the intern to observe the sponsor doing an activity.
- Have the intern do the activity with the supervisor.
- Have the sponsor observe the intern doing the activity.
- Have the intern do the activity on his own.
- Give feedback frequently.

At times, certain steps will need to be repeated or written down, but in general, students will learn best when actively involved in the learning process, not just listening to instructions.

How to Help the Intern on the First Day

Interns will be unfamiliar with the work environment and will need some guidance as to what to expect and what is expected of them. A structured orientation program will help introduce the intern to the business on his first day of work. It will also answer many of the questions interns have on their first day.

Although the orientation of an intern must be tailored to each particular situation, a general orientation would cover many of the questions the intern may have.

What the Intern Will Need to Know

- Where will I sit and work? Is there a place to store my personal belongings?
- What does this business do? Who will I be working with?
- What department and which employees will I be interacting with?
- What is the main purpose of the department?
- What does each person do?
- What are the expectations of the workplace?
- What are the hours? Dress code?
- What are the policies and procedures?
- What should I do if I am going to be late or cannot come into work?
- How does the equipment work?
- What are my tasks and responsibilities?
- What am I expected to do?
- What am I expected to learn?
- What will be your working relationship with me?
- How often will we meet?
- How much will I work independently?
- How will I be supervised?
- Do you have any specific expectations for me?

The orientation checklist in figure 5.1 captures most of the items interns need to know about their internship site. They need to be reassured that asking for a review of some of the information is expected and that they should feel free to bring up anything that might have been missed during the orientation.

What Interns Really Want

Sponsors are grateful to be given tips and techniques for working with their interns. They want them to be successful. And the school, by providing information on the nature of adolescents or what interns want, can help the sponsor not feel as if the responsibility for the internship experience rests solely on their shoulders. A list similar to this has proven to be helpful to many sponsors across the country:

Interns want:

- to be successful in the work environment and to have some of your time and attention;

Sponsor Orientation Checklist

Orientation Checklist

Intern _____ Date _____

Emergency Contact _____

Welcome and Introduction:
- What it means to work at this company

Tour:
- Overall tour of facility
- Complete tour of work area
- Point out fire extinguishers, fire escapes, exits, evacuation routes
- Introductions to staff

The Workplace:
- Rest rooms
- Lunch facility
- Telephones
- Parking
- Where to store personal belongings

The Company:
- Discuss company structure .
- Company values
- Key people in the company
- Type of business, products, services
- Who your customers are
- Other branches or divisions

Workplace Specific:
- Telephone number and address
- Explanation of work schedule
- Hours
- Break times
- Lunch break
- Location of time clock or sign in
- Working with other departments and co-workers.
- Attendance requirements
- Calling in when absent and punctuality

Job Specific:
- How to use the phone
- Supplies, paper, pens, etc.
- Office equipment
- Files
- Job description
- Training plan

Safety Training:
- Stairwell/ fire exits
- Fire extinguishers
- Special hazards
- Accident prevention
- Fire alarms
- Fire Alarm testing

Standards:
- Dress code (clothing, hair, jewelry)
- Work performance (productivity, work habits)
- Company culture (team work, customer service, values)
- Discuss expectation
- Security and confidentiality issues

Company Information:
- Copy of personnel handbook
- Organizational chart
- Telephone directory
- Safety procedures
- Intern physical workplace

Figure 5.1. Sponsor Orientation Checklist

- to be challenged—interns want to work and learn. They want to contribute to the organization and be meaningfully utilized;
- to know what they can expect during their internship. Too often interns feel that they are just given tasks and don't understand how these tasks fit into their learning;
- feedback—interns want to know when they are doing good work or when and how they need to improve;
- to be included—interns want to be part of the team but sometimes they may not know what they need to do to be included. Attending staff meetings and being part of a lunch group will help them feel they are a team member;
- to understand what they need to do—give the intern a detailed explanation when work is assigned to them. There may be times that interns don't know the questions to ask to fully understand what is expected of them;
- a mentor—interns need to have a mentor in the workplace to provide guidance. The best mentor in the world is useless if he or she can't or won't spend the necessary time mentoring. As newcomers, interns may not speak up if they're feeling ignored. The burden of making sure they're okay is on the mentor;
- a place to work—interns need their own chair and workplace. Other staff members need to know what the intern is there to do;
- some help with related expenses—many interns are on a tight personal budget and any help with expenses such as coffee at break times, or special clothing/uniforms would be gratefully accepted.

No matter how much a sponsor has prepared for an intern and how much time is spent with him, there will invariably be times of misunderstanding and even conflict, from a simple problem with time to a larger problem with difficulty following directions and responding to constructive criticism. All sponsors must be prepared to handle conflict with their intern if it comes up.

HANDLING CONFLICT

One of the most important ways the school, via the coordinator, can help support the sponsor is by assisting if conflict arises. And it is possible that conflict will arise at some point in the internship. Many interns may be uncomfortable with conflict and many may not have the skills needed to work through the conflict situation.

Conflicts are a natural part of human relationships. Most adults know that it is better to deal with conflicts than ignore them. We cannot assume that the intern will know this. It will probably fall to the sponsor as supervisor on-site to initiate the resolution process. Interns will respond best if they are able to understand how their behavior is impacting on the business and if they already have a stable, positive relationship with the sponsor.

For example, helping the sponsor understand why saying "Knock off the attitude" is not as helpful as saying "I'm feeling uncomfortable about the way you respond when asked to finish the work you have before you start another task. I think it makes us look unprofessional to our coworkers. What do you think about this? Is there a way we can change this?" This opens the door to a discussion about the intern's self-perception and allows the intern to enter into the conversation and discuss why he or she may be responding in a certain manner. Of course, the coordinator, knowing the personalities of both sponsor and student, may have to have a private conversation with the student about learning how to accept corrections that may not be delivered in the kindest manner. Dealing with various personalities in the workplace is all part of the learning experience.

Usually there are no conflicts, and when they do arise, they can generally be resolved through discussion during seminars or classes or with the program coordinator. If a misunderstanding at a site rises to the level of needing intervention, it is best if the coordinator brings the intern and sponsor together for a three-way discussion.

Interns learn rather quickly that, in the workplace, differences of opinion or misunderstandings are handled quite differently than in the school environment or on the street corner. This is all part of learning what things will be like in the real world after graduation.

When the internship is grounded by a site-specific learning plan, and the intern, sponsor, and coordinator have established a solid relationship, the likelihood of problems developing are reduced and the internship usually runs smoothly. The intern and mentor are busy building their mentoring relationship with the mentor modeling appropriate behavior and supporting the student's learning and the intern reaping the benefit of the mentor's expertise, guidance, and direction.

NOTES

1. Thomas R. Bailey, Katherine L. Hughes, and David Thornton Moore, *Working Knowledge: Work-based Learning and Education Reform* (New York: Routledge, 2004), 184.

2. Dan Conrad and Diane Hedin, *National Assessment of Experiential Education: A Final Report*, report no. ED223765 (St. Paul, MN: Center for Youth Development and Research, 1981), 38.

3. H. Frederick Sweitzer and Mary A. King, *The Successful Internship: Personal, Professional, and Civic Development* (Belmont, CA: Brooks/Cole, 2009), 254.

4. Harvard Graduate School of Education, *Pathways to Prosperity: Meeting the Challenge of Preparing Young Americans for the 21st Century*, report, Harvard Graduate School of Education, February 2011, 20. www.gse.harvard.edu/news_events/features/2011/Pathways_to_Prosperity_Feb2011.pdf.

Chapter Six

Seminars for Reflective Learning

Making Sense of It All

We do not learn from experience . . . we learn from reflecting on experience.

—John Dewey[1]

IMPORTANCE OF REFLECTION

One often-overlooked component of an internship program is a way for students to reflect on their new experiences and learning. Students are continuously growing and developing. Internships give students the opportunity for building their cognitive, practical, and personal/social skills in a real-world environment. However, interns, who are young adults, can benefit from help and guidance in making sense of the changes they are experiencing and the new behaviors expected of them.

In an internship program, reflection is the ability of an intern to step back from an experience and question it from a variety of intellectual and social perspectives. Students have the opportunity to reflect on what they find on the job, ask why it is the way they have found it, how it might be different, and what they have learned.[2] Interns are constantly being exposed to new skills and experiences in the workplace while at the same time they themselves are changing and growing. Interns need to make sense of all this, reflect on themselves and their experiences, and internalize what they are learning.

Some internship programs rely on the student journal as the sole vehicle for student reflection. While this does help the student to reflect on his experiences, it is private with only a teacher or internship coordinator talking with the student about his/her writings. Reflective learning can be more powerful when students are able to share their experiences with other interns and begin to see the similarities and differences in the way others have handled situations. Designing opportunities where students can reflect on their experiences together helps them to:

• Consolidate their problem solving and critical thinking skills learned through achieving the goals and activities of their Individual Learning Plans.

- Make sense of the new workplace experience in moving from student to "employee," being managed or supervised, making decisions, and being a responsible member of a team.
- Build new skills and behaviors that are expected of them in the workplace.
- Become aware of their own personal and social changes as they grow into adulthood.
- Find ways to relate as adult to adult in the workplace.

One student, for example, who interned at an animal hospital, was able to express in his private journal his emotional upset at seeing an animal euthanized. The teacher was able to recommend some books on euthanasia and animal medicine for the student to read. And, at the same time, the student chose to tell his group stories about animal surgeries and express some of his feelings. The teacher then went on to lead a discussion about animal euthanasia.[3]

Giving interns the opportunity to keep a private journal and yet share some of their experiences helps them to learn more about themselves.

Framework for Reflective Learning

A structured approach to reflective learning includes the student journal, a focus on new skills and behaviors, an emphasis on personal development, and an opportunity to learn from others.

Student Journal

The student journal is kept by the student during the internship placement. Writing a journal is private and should not be open to discussion with others as students are encouraged to write about their innermost thoughts and feelings. While good student writing can be part of the personal reflective process, students often only enter factual data about their daily experience in the workplace. Teachers can help guide the students to include their thoughts and feelings about specific topics that can help them reflect on their actions and feelings. The teacher can raise specific questions to help students think about their experiences. These questions can arise from the discussions students bring to the seminars but are only guidance to help them think about their new work experiences and environment.

While specific questions can be suggested in the seminar meeting, the student's writing remains private. Some questions a teacher may ask the interns to address are:

1. Write about a conflict, success, or disappointment you're experiencing at your internship.
2. Describe the expectations you had of this internship when you chose it, and whether those expectations have been met or changed as a result of the actual experience.
3. Describe the internship activity you enjoy the most and the one you enjoy the least.
4. Which of your accomplishments at this internship do you take most pride in?
5. Write about a risk you took in your life or internship or project.

6. Write about a conflict you are having in your life or at the internship from the point of view of the sponsor, internship coordinator, family member, or peer.
7. Discuss what your internship taught you about yourself.
8. What skills and knowledge gained at this internship do you feel you will be able to use in future jobs or educational situations?

The teacher could pose a different question at each seminar to ensure that the student writing does not become repetitive. These questions all challenge the student to address some of the issues where he or she may feel uncomfortable. Journals serve as an outlet of expression of thoughts and feelings that cannot be declared at the work site.[4] Helping the student to focus on some challenging situations helps her gain a deeper understanding of her workplace experiences.

Seminar Content: Real-World Skills

Seminars are the place where the teacher can help guide the learning of the student as she encounters the new and different environment of the workplace. The focus of the seminar should be on developing and strengthening those skills and behaviors that lead to successful job performance. These are not job-specific skills but they are the skills and behaviors that an employer or organization wants to see demonstrated. In a seminar setting the teacher can introduce a framework for these skills and behaviors and help the student to identify what they look like in the workplace. These workplace behaviors are often new to the intern and the best way to internalize them is through reflection and practice. Seminars provide a safe place for the intern to reflect on her behavior in the workplace and practice new workplace skills.

Today's employers have a choice in hiring. So, successful candidates for entry-level positions, whether directly from high school or from a two-year college, need to show that they have those qualities in terms of skills and behaviors that the employer wants. Most companies, whether for-profit, not-for-profit, government agencies, or educational institutions, are looking for similar behaviors for their new hires for entry-level positions. These include:

- Communication
- Teamwork
- Adaptability/flexibility
- Critical thinking/problem solving
- Creativity
- Achievement Focus
- Motivation
- Quality Standards
- Personal Awareness

If the internship program is using Internship Learning Plans, for example, the goals and activities can be structured so that students have the opportunity to build their critical thinking/problem solving, and creativity skills.

Specific definitions and examples of life skills can be introduced to the students in the seminar. With new entrants to the workforce or internships it is best to provide a definition of the skills in both positive and negative terms. This shows the intern what behavior is successful and what is not. Examples of three behaviors—personal awareness, communicating, and team working—written in terms of workplace competencies include the following (see tables 6.1, 6.2, and 6.3).

The competencies are written in behavioral terms so that the student can quickly see what demonstrated behaviors lead to success. For example, the teacher may ask the student to observe the communication of someone in their workplace and identify successful communication skills. The teacher could also ask the student to talk about being part of a team, and this may be in her internship or may be as part of a class project team. Reinforcement of good team behaviors by the teacher can help students become aware of how a successful team works. Once a student is aware of what is specifically expected of her in the workplace, she will be able to act accordingly.

Seminar Process

The seminar is not a typical class where students are at desks and the teacher is at the front of the room. In the seminar the teacher becomes a facilitator who is not judging the students but who is facilitating their learning by posing challenging questions and opening dialogue. Interns are now part of the adult working world and meetings in companies are usually held around a conference table, in a circle group, or even informally in whatever space is available. It is important to reflect this type of environment when meeting with students in a seminar. Seminars can be thought of as the equivalent of a company training session where employees often learn new information as a group but then break into teams or smaller groups to discuss and practice new skills.

However, interns are also teenagers and need a more structured but still informal learning environment as they assess and reflect on their workplace experiences. For seminars to be successful they need to:

- Have a consistent structure so that the student knows what the format is from week to week. Providing transparent structure helps teenagers feel comfortable especially when asked to reflect on new experiences.
- Use icebreakers as a way to encourage individuals to get to know each other, become comfortable with each other, and develop trust.
- Have individual activities that enable the student to learn more about herself. These could be questionnaires or self-assessments. Focus these on behavioral competencies. For example, a questionnaire on individual personality traits or one on personal values will help the student develop skills in personal awareness. Introducing job satisfaction factors and asking students to identify which of the factors motivate them helps them to understand motivation and their own motivational behavior. An individual questionnaire or self-assessment on time management helps students to understand the importance of achievement focus.
- Have group activities that enable students to work together as a team and develop new skills. For example, brainstorming ideas around a specific topic or question, finding group consensus on successful solutions and communicating them to others

Table 6.1. Personal Awareness

Shows interest in understanding self; is open to learning more about self	
Positive Indicators	*Negative Indicators*
• Looks for ways to learn more about self • Is open to new ideas • Accepts feedback and looks for ways to improve • Understands own impact on others • Understands what motivates self • Is aware of cultural similarities and differences • Show an awareness of own emotions	• Shows no interest in self-improvement • Does not want to learn about new ideas • Is not aware of own impact on *others* • Shows no awareness of different cultures • Has no awareness of what motivates him- or herself • Is not able to identify own emotions

Reprinted courtesy of Internship Quest LLC, *Seminar Support Manual*, 2006, p. 3. www.internshipquest.com

Table 6.2. Communicating

Communicates clearly and to the point	
Positive Indicators	*Negative Indicators*
• Speaks clearly • Asks questions to gain information • Knows the difference between open and closed questions • Listens to others • Gains support for ideas though enthusiasm • Keeps others informed • Makes positive statements about work and others	• Mumbles • Does not ask any questions • Does not listen and shows no interest in others • Talks negatively about work and others • Does not tell others what he or she is doing

Reprinted courtesy of Internship Quest LLC, *Seminar Support Manual*, 2006, p. 3. www.internshipquest.com

Table 6.3. Teamwork

Works willingly in a team, understands own contribution to team success	
Positive Indicators	*Negative indicators*
• Works willingly in a team • Can identify own role and role of others • Gives information to other *team members* • Treats individual team members the way they want to be treated • Shows a willingness to help other *team members* • Shows awareness of own actions and impact on the team	• Shows no interest in being part of a team • Has no awareness of different *roles of team members* • Does not share information with team members • Is insensitive to others • Ignores request for help from others • Speaks negatively about other *team members*

Reprinted courtesy of Internship Quest LLC, *Seminar Support Manual*, 2006, p. 4. www.internshipquest.com

help students build skills in creativity and communication. In addition, group or team discussions about a work-related problem or incident, with the teacher's guidance allows the intern to reflect on her behavior and understand different ways of handling the situation.

- Provide a way for the intern to communicate her learning from the seminar activities. This can be accomplished simply by asking each intern what they learned from the specific seminar activities and topics.
- Provide a way for the intern to summarize her experience. This could be through guidance in writing a résumé and a summary of the internship for entry on the transcript.

Seminars not only help students to reflect on their learning and their new experiences in a safe environment but they also give students ways to identify and define the new skills and behaviors they have learned. Seminars are a critical component of any internship program and need to be part of any internship experience.

Example of a Typical Seminar Plan

- Icebreaker (or warm-up) group activity;
- Work week and reflection discussion: What did you do this week at your work? What did you like? What went well? Were there any problems? Is there anything that you would have done differently?
- Individual or group activity such as self-assessment or team activity;
- Teacher-led discussion about the activity outcomes and what they mean;
- Learns and likes: Each student tells the group what they learned and what they liked about the seminar;
- Journal-entry question for the week to help guide the intern in reflecting on new learning;
- Plan for the work week: Each student identifies what plan they have for the coming week at work.

Building High Self-Efficacy

Self-efficacy is an individual's belief about his or her ability to perform a task.[5] Individuals with high self-efficacy believe that they can perform a specific task (even if the task is new to them) but individuals with low self-efficacy doubt their ability. Internships give students the opportunity to build high self-efficacy as they take on and complete new and different tasks in the workplace. However, students and new employees, for example, need a structured environment and support as they begin to build their belief in their own abilities.

While the strongest influence on the intern in the workplace may be the supervisor or team leader, the teacher can have a major role in helping students to build high self-efficacy. As the facilitator or leader of the weekly seminars, teachers set challenging questions for the student to address in her journal and can then have a one-to-one discussion about how the student addressed the question. Teachers also give support when the student describes tackling new tasks in the workplace. Teachers can also affirm the intern's demonstration of new behaviors and life skills. As students develop high self-efficacy they will be able to handle new and challenging tasks in the future, whether in college or in the workplace.

Coaching to Build New Skills: The Mentor as Coach

One aspect of the role of mentoring is being a coach to the intern. The sponsor may be mentoring the intern but it is often the day-to-day supervisor that can become a coach. Many organizations encourage their supervisors, managers, and team leaders to be good coaches for their employees. Coaching is one of the most powerful ways to help an individual grow and develop. And students are familiar with the coaching relationship through various school activities.

Whatever adult in the workplace takes on the role of coach to the intern, he will need guidance from the teacher or internship program director. Many of the sponsors/supervisors may not have experience in supervising or even coaching teenagers. One way the school can help build a strong relationship with the sponsoring organization is to provide guidelines for coaching. An organization benefits from encouraging their supervisors to coach an intern as it helps the supervisor to build valuable coaching skills that can be used in the future.

The teacher or internship program coordinator can outline the skills the intern needs to develop by identifying the behaviors focused on in the seminars. For example, the supervisor coach can help the intern build personal awareness by asking the intern about her personality traits if a personality assessment was part of the seminar. The supervisor has firsthand experience of how any personality trait may be seen in the workplace. Conscientiousness, for example, can easily be discussed, using the intern's timekeeping and completion of tasks as examples.

The supervisor coach is also best placed to help the intern focus on career interests. Helping the intern to identify how her interests and strengths can help guide her in a career choice or college major will enable her to write a stronger résumé. It is important for the coach to link his coaching sessions with the skills being developed and reinforced in the internship seminars, and this may be done by building a formal coaching relationship with the intern.

Coaches provide the teenager with an adult relationship and often can be the person who can keep the student on track for college and career. But coaches need guidance from the teacher or internship program coordinator so that the coaching relationship can be beneficial both to the intern and to the coach.

SEMINARS ONLINE

Seminars are the component of the internship program that enable the students to reflect and consolidate their learning. It is also where students learn from each other,

---

BUILDING PERSONAL AWARENESS: COACHING GUIDELINES

In the seminars, the student has been completing self-assessment exercises focused on building her personal awareness by looking at, for example, her personality profile, personal values, and motivation. The intern's workplace supervisor can schedule a coaching session and reinforce the intern's learning about herself and begin to help the intern to link her personal awareness to specific workplace behaviors.

The coach can ask:

- Tell me about your internship placement: What do you like about it? What work do you do? What has gone well? What has not gone so well?
- What is your personality profile? What do you think the personality profiles of your teammates, boss, others in the workplace are? Do you think they are similar to or different than you? Why? How do you think your personality helps you get on with others?
- What are your values? How do you think you use your values in the workplace? What do you think the values are of the others in your workplace? Are they similar or different to yours?
- What things are important to you? What makes you work hard or want to complete a task? What will motivate you to do a good job in your workplace? What would you change in your workplace so that you could work better?

At the end of the session, ask the student:
- What have you learned, so far, about yourself? What have you learned about others?
- What are your plans for the next few weeks at work? Will you do anything differently? Will you try something new? What would that be?

Adapted courtesy of Internship Quest LLC, *Seminar Support Manual* 2006, p. 57. www.internshipquest.com

---

build trust, and practice new skills and behaviors. Seminars should be held face-to-face so that students experience firsthand differing views, practice new skills with others, and get to know their intern colleagues.

However, many schools today are moving to the delivery of online learning and there is an opportunity for quality seminars also to be part of the online experience. Online platforms are interactive and not only allow for students to post and respond to discussion questions but also have features that allow teachers to facilitate real-time group activities. One example of incorporating online learning with face-to-face learning is to develop the seminars as a blended component of an online internship program. Meeting once face-to-face every other week, for example, with teacher-guided content and facilitated discussions online the other week, can combine both the benefits of online and face-to-face learning.

Whatever seminar delivery is used, it is important to ensure that the seminars are structured, have ample opportunities for student interactions, and reinforce the positive learning experience of internships.

Reflective learning is a critical component for a successful internship learning experience. Reflection gives context to the intern's experiences and enables him or her to gain an understanding of a variety of work-related issues. A structured seminar ensures the student is able to internalize the learning from the workplace and to build new and effective behaviors that will lead to success. Seminars also provide a framework for interns to move from the world of student to the world of adult by giving them the space to begin to behave like adults in the real world.

NOTES

1. John Dewey, *How We Think: A Restatement of the Relation of Reflective Thinking to the Educative Process* (Boston, MA: D.C. Heath, 1933).

2. Thomas R. Bailey, Katherine L. Hughes, and David Thornton Moore, *Working Knowledge: Work-based Learning and Education Reform* (New York: Routledge, 2004), 198.

3. Bailey, Hughes, and Moore, *Working Knowledge*, 205–6.

4. Bailey, Hughes, and Moore, *Working Knowledge*, 205.

5. Ricky W. Griffin and Gregory Moorehead, *Organizational Behavior: Managing People and Organizations*, 8th ed. (New York: Houghton Mifflin, 2007), 66.

Chapter Seven

Evaluating Internship Learning

Putting It All Together

Exhibitions of internship work were high points of the year. Younger students who attend exhibitions . . . begin talking about what they'll do when it's their turn to do an internship; and mentors, who are sometimes in the school for the first time, see some of its finest moments.

—Eliot Levine[1]

Schools that support internships often voice the concern that assessing and measuring the learning of an internship experience can often be vague and incomplete. Some schools are concerned that much of the learning occurs at the placement site and so traditional school-based assessment is difficult to do. Other schools share the concern that the learning is often passed off to the internship supervisor. Therefore schools indicate that students are unable to earn credit for work and learning accomplished at the placement site as there is often no evidence of learning or academic goals met.

The concern about compromising assessment integrity often holds schools back from developing and implementing internships. Many schools want to ensure that there is robust assessment and evaluation of learning for all classes in which students earn credit. This can be especially true when credit fulfills any graduation requirement.

THE IMPORTANCE OF FEEDBACK

Today's students are used to getting immediate feedback. They constantly get feedback from their friends online through their Facebook account, use instant messaging to communicate, and always want to know that they have done well. This is true in school as well as in the workplace. Designing an assessment process that enables the interns to get feedback on an ongoing basis will ensure that they will stay engaged with their learning. Weekly seminars that focus on workplace learning, individual online structured discussions and/or one-on-one meetings with the internship coordinator or sponsor are some ways a school can build feedback opportunities. And these opportunities allow for the teacher/coordinator or sponsor to give both positive and constructive feedback. Ongoing feedback that communicates clearly defined benchmarks for success, and the metrics and milestones of measuring that success, helps the students to stay focused, especially when they might feel challenged in their placement.

This chapter looks at ways schools can set robust learning standards and measure and assess academic and workplace skills that the student learns in his internship learning experience.

PERFORMANCE-BASED ASSESSMENT

Since internships are experiences in which the student learns in the real world, any assessment of learning needs to be based on evidence gathered from the placement.

Performance-based assessment, therefore, is the evaluation of a student's evidence of accomplishment of curriculum goals that demonstrate achievement. While the goals reflect the student's learning in the workplace, they are set by the teachers and the schools and reflect both standards common to all internship learning as well as the individual internship placement. Evidence of achievement can include informational briefs, oral presentations, open-ended problem solutions, hands-on problem solutions, and authentic tasks that show what a student can do.

There are two types of assessments or evaluation for internships—ongoing and final. Section one of this chapter looks at ongoing assessments that are done as students progress through their internship. Section two looks at final assessments that are done at the completion of the internship experience. Sample rubrics for each final assessment method are included in section three. These examples can be adapted by a school and tailored to meet specific program evaluation needs. Most quality internship programs use both ongoing and final assessments.

In order to be a robust evaluation of a student's work and learning, whatever method is used, teachers need to agree about the outcomes expected and the standards for success.

> It is crucial that we develop a more sophisticated assessment system that incorporates more meaningful assessment data at the school level, such as portfolio assessments, demonstrations, oral presentations, and applied projects.[2]

SECTION ONE: ONGOING ASSESSMENT

Common Goals and Activities

Each internship placement will have a number of goals or activities that are common or uniform. No matter if a student is an intern in a hospital, for example, or at a bank, there are common activities each can complete. These focus on helping the student to learn the specifics about his placement field, specifics about the organization's structure and the career opportunities, and understanding of individual career progression.

These goals also enable the student to reflect on his experience and how the internship strengthens the résumé and transcript.

Three examples of common or uniform goals, activities, and possible assessment and evaluation include:

Student Journal

Goal: To keep a journal for each day of the internship so that the student has an opportunity to reflect on his daily experience.

Activity: A student enters his personal reactions, likes, dislikes, high points, low points, surprises, disappointments, etc., at the end of the day or when there is a lull in the day's activities.

Learning: These entries help the student to reflect on his experience. Journal entries can be done as a paper journal or electronically in an online file. It is helpful if the teacher sets specific topics for the student to write about in his entry so that all interns have similar guidelines.

Evaluation: Private discussions with the intern about his journal writing will indicate the quality of writing and depth of understanding of new experiences.

Career-Path Research

Goal: To become aware of career opportunities, educational preparation, and training needed so that the student has an understanding of what is required to work in a specific field.

Activity: Each student interviews three to five people at his internship site who perform different jobs so that the student becomes aware of career opportunities, educational preparation, and training needed for work in this field.

Learning: Here it is helpful if the teacher provides each student with specific interview questions as well as encouraging each to use his own questions. Students can structure these interviews as a journalist, for example, or they may summarize the interviews in an essay format. They can submit these interviews in paper form individually, or as a project summarizing all the interviews, or electronically as a journalistic blog.

> *Just being around really experienced people and knowing how they got into the field was great for me.*
>
> —*Student Intern*

Evaluation: Review of the submission will indicate quality of writing and the completion of the required interviews.

Student Intern Thank-You Letter

Goal/Activity: Write a thank-you letter to the intern sponsor.

Learning: Thank-you letters are important in the world of work. Often candidates who write a thank-you note to a company will get called back for a second interview. Interns should be encouraged to write a thank-you letter to their sponsor thanking her for the opportunity to work there as an intern. Including a description of some of the things the intern learned as a result of the internship will help ensure that the sponsor stays connected to the school and will again offer an internship opportunity. Many sponsors themselves have benefited from an internship early in their career and want to offer the same learning opportunity to young people.

Evaluation: Review of the thank-you letter indicates quality of writing and learning during the internship experience.

Although students will be in different placements, teachers can establish specific guidelines for these activities so students are working to similar goals. Individual assessments can be done as each student completes each activity or the evaluation of achievement can become part of the student's portfolio or presentation.

Individual Internship Goals and Activities

In addition to these common goals and activities, each intern will have goals and activities specific to his placement. An Internship Learning Plan, which is done for each placement, should have specific activities for the intern to complete. These may include such activities as:

Hotel Placement
Goal: To understand how a hotel reservations system works.
Activity: Make a flowchart of how a reservations system works in a hotel.
Evaluation: Present the flowchart to the sponsor, seminar, or class and assess the intern's logical organization of material.

Hospital Children's Unit Placement
Goal: To understand the importance of in-hospital activity for young patients.
Activity: Obtain children's books from the hospital library and read to children either individually or in a group.
Evaluation: Present the choice of selected books to the sponsor, seminar or class and assess the intern's understanding of age appropriate material.

Farm or Ranch Assistant
Goal: To learn about and identify the equipment used on the farm.
Activity: Using a camera, photograph the farm equipment, mount the photos for display, and name each piece of equipment and its purpose.
Evaluation: Presentation of the photo exhibition to the sponsor, seminar, or class, and assess the ability of the intern to organize material for communication to others.

Internship Learning Plans give the teacher an opportunity to focus on specific learning in an individual placement as well as to develop goals and activities in different student learning styles. These plans give teachers the opportunity evaluate learning that is hands-on as well as academic. They also allow one-on-one assessment.

Attendance

Attendance can also be part of an ongoing assessment. Regular attendance is vital for the student to maximize his learning from the internship experience. Any pattern of nonattendance may indicate that the student is having some problems. Reviewing attendance allows a teacher to pick up any problems early so that student can continue to benefit from the internship experience.

SECTION TWO: FINAL ASSESSMENT

The final assessment of a student's work and learning is usually done at the end of the internship placement.

Following are six performance-based assessments that enable students to demonstrate their learning against robust standards:

1. Student portfolio
2. Student presentation
3. Student exhibit of the internship experience
4. Individual one-on-one assessment of learning
5. Student self-evaluation
6. Sponsor evaluation of intern

Student Portfolio

A student portfolio for internships is the vehicle for the student to bring together in one place evidence of all of his learning. Many colleges today require students to establish and keep a portfolio of their learning each year. Most students keep their portfolios electronically so that they can update and amend as necessary. The electronic portfolio can be assessed and discussed throughout the year or at the end of each semester. Using a portfolio for all the work done in an internship helps the college-bound student as well as the career-focused student to summarize their learning and provides a basis for the student to discuss their internship experience with an admissions counselor and a potential employer.

The portfolio should include:

- Examples of the tasks completed by the intern at her placement. These can be those tasks assigned by the workplace sponsor or supervisor and the goals and activities in the individual internship learning plan.

- Evidence of Completion of problem solving/critical thinking goals

- Evidence of problem solving and critical thinking are vital for a student's success in her career or higher education. With a quality curriculum, internships give students the opportunity to learn and apply these skills in the real world. Two examples of problem solving/critical thinking goals are:

1. Hospital Volunteer Office (Data Management) Placement
   Goal: To understand the importance of keeping accurate information
   Activity: Organize a system to keep track of volunteers so that volunteers can be contacted and scheduled in a timely manner.
   Evaluation: A database system (or other system) of volunteers, their addresses, phone numbers, and preferred time which can be used to schedule their time, and a one-month record of time for volunteers in your work cycle. The system shows evidence of organization, problem identification, and solution.

2. Landscaping Placement
   Goal: Understand and demonstrate how all the separate elements of landscaping fit together as a whole.
   Activity: Design of a landscaping project including diagram of plants and placement and diagram for water delivery system.
   Evaluation: A diorama or drawing (electronic or paper) of plantings and water system with a written explanation of the system. The diorama shows evidence of logical thinking and planning, problem identification, and solution.

• Examples of Use of Technology

Technology is a critical part of any workplace or higher learning environment. An intern should have the opportunity to use and develop technology skills in the workplace, school computer lab, or own laptop. An example of the use of technology for all interns would be the completion of Uniform Goal 2 using the Internet to research literature in the field and presenting findings.

• Examples of Career Skills

Employers, whether they are for profit companies, non-profit, or volunteer organizations, expect their employees to demonstrate appropriate behaviors in the workplace. These may include teamwork, customer/client focus, and communication and achievement focus. Although these behaviors are often learned in the workplace, evidence of a student's accomplishment can be presented in his portfolio.

Evidence of behaviors could include:

1. An evaluation by the sponsor of the student's performance against these workplace behaviors that will provide feedback to the student as well as evidence of skill development.
2. Seminars that use skill development material and worksheets can provide evidence of learning in these areas. The material can be included in the portfolio.

3. Specific questions can be asked of the student so that he can demonstrate learning in these areas. For example, a question about teamwork could be:

"Tell me about a time when you were part of the team. What was the team and what was your role? How did the team divide the work that had to be done? Was there anyone on that team who did not pull his weight? What did you do about it? What did you learn from being part of this team?"

Students could include written answers to such questions in their portfolio.

Student Presentation

The student's presentation could be a formal presentation to an advisory board of teachers, administrators, or sponsors, or it could be to a more informal audience including teachers, peers, and sponsors. The student would be expected to use audiovisual aids such as PowerPoint, project boards, handouts, and pictures. The presentation should take about twenty minutes, with additional time for question and answers, and include:

> *I was so grateful to have the opportunity to present. I now realize the value of teaching others rather than just making money of the stock market. . . . I now have another career option.*
>
> *—Student Intern*

Introduction

This would include the student's personal reason for choosing the internship, an indication of what she expected the internship to be like, and a summary of the reality; the organization or agency of her placement including its history, description of what the organization does, and its purpose or mission.

Body of the Presentation

This would include the intern role and what he accomplished. Here the intern could give real examples of projects, tasks, and added value.

Evidence of Learning

Here the student has the opportunity to focus on specific learning and to show specific evidence of what was learned. This could include:

- Problem Solving:
  The student could give an example of a project or activity in which he/she had to apply problem solving skills. Here an assessor might be looking for "big picture" awareness, examples of gathering and sorting information, and reaching a conclusion.

- Teamwork:
  The student would show evidence of working in a team by describing a task or project on which a team worked. She would show an awareness of her role in the team, how obstacles were overcome, how any difficult members were handled, and what she learned about teamwork.

- Client Focus:
  Many organizations, whether for profit, non-profit, or volunteer agencies, serve a client base. Here the student could give examples of face-to-face customer service, an awareness of different client/customer needs, and examples of excellent customer/client service.

- Personal Development:
  Here the student has the opportunity to show evidence of insight into her own behavior in the workplace. This insight would have been gathered through reflection, discussion in the seminar, and feedback from the sponsor, teachers, and peers.

- Career Awareness:
  The internship experience should give the student a clearer awareness of career options. Here the assessor would be looking for the student so show an awareness of the future either in a career or in higher education.

Conclusion

A clear and succinct summary should close the presentation with questions and answers.

Student Exhibition

If an internship program is used, for example, for all seniors, the school may find an exhibition an appropriate part of their assessment. Exhibits communicate the accomplishments of the intern not only to teachers but also to peers and students in lower grades. An exhibit also enables the interns to talk about their experience in an informal setting and build enthusiasm for the program in students in other grades.

Sponsors are invited to the exhibit, which is often set up in the school's gym, and here they are then able to network with other sponsors and meet other interns.

Exhibits are also an excellent way to ensure parental involvement, as they would be invited to view all the exhibits and talk with students and teachers. They are also a way to fully involve and stay connected with the sponsors, which can ensure future internship placements.

Content

Students would use a project board with visuals to show the work of their organization and their accomplishments. The intern would talk about their experience informally to everyone who visits their exhibit. They would also be expected to answer questions from teachers, students, parents, and guests. In discussions the intern should cover:

- The mission, purpose, product, and/or service of their sponsor organization
- The intern's role in the organization
- Examples of what the intern did in their placement
- Examples of what the intern learned about the organization, industry, customers/clients, self, etc.
- What the intern most liked about the placement
- What was learned about careers
- What impact the placement has had on the intern's future

Individual Assessment

Smaller internship programs may choose to assess a student's learning through interview. However, the interview needs to be focused on what the student learned in her placement and be evidence based.

Three examples of evidence-based questions, which uncover learning, are:

- Problem solving: The assessment here enables the student to demonstrate that she has been able to collect data, analyze, explore options, and reach a conclusion.

  Give me an example of a problem or project you worked on in your placement where you had to collect information. What was the problem and what information did you need to collect? What did you do with this information? Were there any differences in the information you collected? How did you handle these discrepancies? What was the outcome of your investigations? Did you draw any conclusions? If so, what were they?

- Communication: The assessment here enables the student to demonstrate that she is able to present information and ideas clearly, is able to gain support for her ideas, to demonstrate enthusiasm, and to listen.

  Can you tell me about a time in your placement when you had to convince someone to do something. This may have been a coworker, someone in the internship program, a customer, or client. What did you need to convince that person to do? What did you say to that person? (Probe here to help the student be specific.) How did that person respond? Was it easy or difficult to convince this person? Why?

- Team working: The assessment here demonstrates if the student understands teamwork, how her role on the team contributes to the team's success and if she understands options when dealing with a reluctant team member.

  Tell me about a time when you were part of the team. What was the team and what was your role? How did the team divide the work that had to be done? Was there anyone on the team that did not pull their weight? What did you do about it? What did you learn being part of this team?

Students can be asked to write a response to the questions rather than responding orally. In this case, the assessor can review the written responses and the examples given.

Student Self-Evaluation

It is important to ask the student to evaluate his internship experience. Through the evaluation, the student will highlight what worked well and what may need to be improved. This is important to know and be addressed as the school moves forward with the relationship with the sponsor. The evaluation also gives insight into the student's learning and what may need to be strengthened. Student evaluations can take the form of short-answer questions, open questions, or ratings.

Sponsor Evaluation of Intern

Sponsors are among those who get to know best how the student behaves and performs in the workplace. And sponsors have criteria and standards on which they evaluate employees. It is helpful, especially to the intern, if a sponsor is able to give feedback to the student throughout his placement. It is also helpful to the school and the intern if the sponsor gives an overall evaluation of the intern against similar criteria used for the evaluation of employees. Often this evaluation will highlight the strengths and areas for development so that the intern can move forward and achieve success in the workplace. It is important that the evaluation dimensions are linked to the behaviors identified in the student intern seminars so that these positive workplace behaviors are reinforced throughout the student's placement.

SECTION THREE: MEASUREMENT RUBRICS

Whether a school or teacher decides to assess the learning of the intern as she progresses through the internship, assess them at the completion of the placement, or both, it is critical that standards for evaluation are developed before the student begins

Student Portfolio of Best Work

Introduction to the Portfolio includes: 1. Reason for portfolio 2. Organization of portfolio	Example of Best Work 1. Why this is an example of the student's best work 2. The work in detail 3. What was learned by doing this work 4. Why is this considered quality work
Example of Problem Solving 1. What was the problem/project/issue 2. The steps taken to investigate 3. The steps taken to analyze research findings 4. Conclusion reached	Example of Work Reflecting Growth 1. What is the work 2. How does it show that the student has grown or improved
Career Awareness 1. What was learned about career and career options from this placement 2. What are the student's career goals	
Adapted from Internship Quest, LLC. *Evaluating Internships and Service learning* pp. 9-10; 2008 www.internshipquest.com	

Figure 7.1.   Student Portfolio of Best Work

her internship. It is also critical that clear standards for success are communicated to students so that they themselves can measure their success along the way. The student intern is learning about the world of work and that the realistic assessment of performance is vital to job success.

Student Portfolio

A student portfolio may include all the work the student has done in his placement and related activities or the teacher may ask the student to include only examples of his best work, an example of problem solving, and a piece of work that has shown how the student has grown or improved in his internship. Figure 7.1 is an example of what might be included in a student portfolio of best work. Figure 7.2 is an example of an assessment rubric for a student portfolio.

Assessment of Student Portfolio

		1	2	3	4
Content	Quality of evidence and examples used, awareness of interrelationships, clear facts				
Analysis	Evidence of reflection, evaluation of evidence, reaching conclusions				
Career Awareness	Relationship between internship/service learning and career/further education goals, use of technology, evidence of teamwork				
Communication	Clear organization, attention to potential audience for portfolio, style, writing, use of vocabulary, evidence of use of technology to research and communicate				

Assessment Key—Portfolio Rubric

4. Excellent	Fully achieves the purposes of the portfolio, demonstrates broad range of concepts and content, provides insights, communicates effectively
3. Good	Accomplishes most of the portfolio tasks, shows good understanding of concepts and content, realistic evaluation of own work, communicates effectively although may have mechanic errors
2. Basic	Does not achieve important purpose of portfolio, shows gaps in major understanding, career goals unclear, superficial evaluation of own work, lack organization in communication
1. No Evidence	Portfolio provides no evidence of completion of goals; no examples of best work
	Reprinted courtesy of Internship Quest, LLC. *Evaluating Internships and Service Learning* pp. 10-11; 2008 www.internshipquest.com

Figure 7.2. Assessment Rubric for Student Portfolio

Student Presentation

The assessment can include how well the presentation was organized, how clear were any audiovisuals, how the student presented herself, evidence of career options of interest to the student, and how well the student handled questions and answers. Figure 7.3 is an example of an assessment rubric for the student presentation.

Student Presentation Assessment Rubric

Content	1	2	3	4	5
Introduction: personal introduction; reason for choosing placement, purpose of presentation					
Body: clear statement of main points, clear examples of problem solving/teamwork/client focus/personal development					
Organization: logical flow of ideas					
Conclusion: clear summary of learning					
Reflection: clear evidence of reflective learning					
Communication					
Audio/visual aids, graphics: supports presentation; appropriate form of communication					
Non-verbal: eye contact, posture, poise					
Verbal: clarity, volume, rate of delivery					
Dress: neat, appropriate dress					
Career Awareness					
Link to future: evidence of career options; evidence of how learning can be used in the future					
Question and Answer					
Impromptu skills: fluent, confident, answers question easily					
Quality of responses: evidence of knowledge, responds directly to the questions					
Key: 1= poor: 5= excellent Totals: 50–60 excellent; 45–50 Good, 35–45 Fair, 25–35 Needs major improvement, Under 25 Poor					
Reprinted courtesy of Internship Quest, LLC. *Evaluating Internships and Service Learning* p. 13; 2008 www.internshipquest.com					

Figure 7.3. Student Presentation Assessment Rubric

Student Exhibit

Specific criteria for success need to be established and communicated to the students before they begin to prepare their exhibit. These can include the quality of any audio-visuals, the ability of the student to talk about specific examples of her learning, how well the student uses the time allotted, and how the student demonstrates knowledge about the placement organization, sector, or industry. Figure 7.4 is an example of a student exhibition rubric.

Student Exhibition Assessment

Exhibit Criteria	1	2	3	4
Exhibit is clear, engaging and appropriate				
Audio/Visuals/technology supports exhibit and are clear and engaging				
Student demonstrates enthusiasm and confidence about placement				
Student talks about specific examples of learning				
Student demonstrates understanding and knowledge about placement organization and industry				
Student answers questions knowledgeably and thoroughly				
Student speaks clearly				
Student makes eye contact with individual and/or audience				
Student is well prepared				
Student uses technology or audio/visuals to enhance discussions				
Student uses time effectively				
Key: 1 = needs improvement; 2 = fair exhibit; 3 = good exhibit; 4 = excellent exhibit				
Reprinted courtesy of Internship Quest, LLC. *Evaluating Internships and Service Learning*				

Figure 7.4. Student Exhibition Rubric

Individual Assessment

When assessing a student individually the assessor needs to carefully listen to ensure that the intern is giving real examples to explain his answer. The assessor may ask questions to get clarification of what the student is saying. It is important that the assessor takes notes that indicate what the student has said when giving his examples. The purpose of an individual assessment is to enable the intern to demonstrate that there is evidence that will show how the criteria have been met.

Students can be asked to write a response to the questions rather than responding orally. In this case, the assessor can review the written responses and the examples given. Figure 7.5 is an example of an individual assessment rubric.

Individual Assessment Rating Scale

Rating Scale: After the assessor has listened (or reviewed the written answers) to the questions he/she could use the following scale on which to rate the student's learning:	
4. Above acceptable standard	(Here the student gives very good examples which are strong and positive and shows insight into own behaviors and learning)
3. Acceptable standard	(Here the student gives examples being asked for and shows some insight into own behaviors and learning)
2. Below acceptable standard	(Here the student may give examples but shows no understanding of behavior or learning)
1. No Evidence	(Here the student is unable to give any examples)
Reprinted courtesy of Internship Quest, LLC. *Evaluating Internships and Service Learning* p. 17; 2008 www.internshipquest.com	

Figure 7.5.   Individual Assessment Rubric

Student Self-Evaluation

The questions used on a student evaluation form can give the school insight into the student view of the program and can lead to improvement. Figure 7.6 is an example of a student self-evaluation form.

Student Self Evaluation

Student:	Sponsor Name:
Title:	Date:

1. Did you like this internship?   Yes   No

2. What skills did you learn and what insights did you gain from this internship?

3. What didn't you like about this internship?

4. Relative to other internships you have taken, how would you rate this one?
   Excellent 1   2   3   4   5   Poor
   Why?

5. How would you rate your own performance?
   Excellent 1   2   3   4   5   Poor
   Why?

6. Did the learning experience match the description? Explain.

7. Would you recommend this internship to other students? Why, or why not?

   This is your chance to tell us how this experience could be improved.

Adapted from Internship Quest, LLC *Student Handbook* pp 16–17.   www.internshipquest.com

Figure 7.6.   Student Self-Evaluation

Sponsor Evaluation of Intern

Any form used for a sponsor evaluation needs to reflect both what the school and the sponsor expects the student to have learned. Figure 7.7 is an example of a sponsor evaluation form.

ONLINE ASSESSMENT

Many schools today are moving forward with online learning, using a variety of platforms. Features of these platforms include the ability of students to post discussion documents, which can be read and commented on by other students as well as teachers; submission of any written assignments, which can then be assessed and graded with feedback to the student; discussion boards; uploads of videos created by students; and real-time discussions. Using online platforms for learning and assessments can help the school organize and manage an internship program. Online assessment gives continuous feedback to students and helps them track their success in their internship.

Sponsor Evaluation

		4	3	2	1	N/E
A.	Personal Awareness	4	3	2	1	N/E
	1. Is open to new ideas	4	3	2	1	N/E
	2. Accepts feedback and looks for ways to improve	4	3	2	1	N/E
	3. Shows an awareness of own emotions	4	3	2	1	N/E
B.	Communication	4	3	2	1	N/E
	1. Listens to others	4	3	2	1	N/E
	2. Asks questions to gain information	4	3	2	1	N/E
	3. Gains support for ideas through enthusiasm	4	3	2	1	N/E
C.	Team Working	4	3	2	1	N/E
	1. Shows willingness to help other team members	4	3	2	1	N/E
	2. Works willingly in a team	4	3	2	1	N/E
	3. Shows awareness of own actions and impact on the team	4	3	2	1	N/E

Rating Scale		
4	Above acceptable standard	Shows positive behaviors all the time
3	Acceptable standard	Shows positive behaviors most of the time
2	Below acceptable standard	Needs to show more positive than negative behaviors; needs some personal development
1	Significantly below acceptable standard	Show significant negative behaviors; strong development is needed on addressing negative behaviors and broadening positive behaviors
N/E	No Evidence	No evidence of either positive or negative behaviors. Adapted from Internship Quest, LLC. *Sponsor Handbook* p. 16 www.internshipquest.com
Adapted from Internship Quest, LLC *Sponsor Handbook*, p. 16. www.internshipquest.com		

Figure 7.7.   Sponsor Evaluation of Intern

NOTES

1. Eliot Levine, "The Rigors and Rewards of Internships," *Educational Leadership* 68, no. 1 (September 2010): 47.

2. Association for Supervision and Curriculum Development, "The ASCD High School Reform Proposal," *ASCD News and Issues: The Legislative Agenda*, 2006. www.ascd.org/ASCD/pdf/newsandissues/High%20School%20Reform%20One%20Page%20Summary.pdf.

Chapter Eight

The Predictable Stages of Internships
No Surprises

Early awareness of the ebb and flow inherent in an internship may decrease the likelihood that challenges will overwhelm interns.

—Joel F. Diambra[1]

This chapter illustrates the stages that interns might experience as they work through the internship experience. There are examples of some common behaviors and phases that might be expected over the course of the internship placement and some tips and techniques to handle these behaviors when they occur to ensure that the student's experience as an intern is a successful one.

THE PREDICTABLE STAGES OF AN INTERNSHIP

Students who complete an internship, whether in a business setting, a non-profit organization, or volunteer agency, often say that this real-world learning was the most valuable experience they had in their school career. Many students say that in their role as an intern they learned about what career path to pursue—or to avoid—and what employers and adults in the workplace expected of them. And, most importantly, they learned about themselves and what they have to contribute to the world of work.

However, in order for an internship to be a success for a student, we need to see the experience through her eyes. Internships ask students to go to an unfamiliar place, to meet and work with new people, to add value to the business or organization, and to learn new skills. This can seem daunting to many. It is not surprising, then, if we see some behaviors, that if left unchecked, could lead to a less than successful experience.

Every intern and internship experience is different, depending on the intern's unique personality, skills, interests, and learning style. All interns pass through a number of stages as they develop from students who know little about the world of work to ones who are gaining workplace skills and adding value to their sponsor's organization. Some interns are able to navigate through these stages more easily than others. It is the coordinator's job to be aware of these stages, feelings, and behaviors, and to address them to ensure that the internship experience is as successful as possible.

The stages described and illustrated next are based on three works: Sweitzer and King's *The Successful Internship: Personal, Professional, and Civic Development*;[2] Inskter and Ross's *The Internship as Partnership: A Handbook for Campus-Based Coordinators and Advisors*;[3] and Pamela Myers Kiser's *The Human Services Internship: Getting the Most from Your Experience*.[4]

Although these publications are written for college internship programs, we have found through experience that the theory and basic stages described can be adapted successfully to secondary- and community-college-level interns. The college-level intern is expected to read and progress through the various stages independently. Secondary and community college students need help not only in understanding the stages they pass through but even in describing their feelings and identifying situations.

It can be frustrating for the sponsors and internship coordinators to deal with students reaching different stages at different times, but this is the natural ebb and flow of the internship experience and to ignore it is to deny students an opportunity to gain the most they can from all aspects of the experience. The best thing to do is to be prepared, to understand that all of the stages are normal, and to help the students understand and grow by encouraging them to reflect on these new experiences, what they are learning about the career area of their internship, the work they are doing, the real-world skills they are gaining, and most importantly themselves.

If interns do not resolve the issues in one stage, they will have problems moving to the next one. They may even backslide to an earlier stage because original issues have not been totally resolved.

Most young adults have very little experience identifying, let alone describing, problem issues, conflicts, and feelings they may be experiencing. Too often they think they are the only ones feeling this way or thinking these thoughts. Even the descriptive titles given to the stages are not words that are familiar to young people in this context, for they have spent their lives in school, not learning in the real world. For an intern, everything is new and it can be very anxiety provoking.

STAGE ONE: ANTICIPATION

Even before the interview and final placement has been completed, most interns are into the anticipation stage. Perhaps they have talked with former interns or attended an end-of-year presentation by students completing their senior projects or internships. They see the upcoming internship experience as different from sitting in the classroom and approach it with eagerness and hope but also with a sense of anxiety.

The student's anxiety may take the form of "what ifs." A student may begin to wonder "what if the staff doesn't like me; what if no one wants to eat lunch with me; what if I have to deal with customers who are difficult; what if I make mistakes; what if I can't keep up with the work."

Selena's Expectations

Before her internship with a pediatrician began, Selena was overly concerned about what clothing would be appropriate to wear, if her collection of jewelry and large earrings would be okay, what shoes would be most comfortable, and on and on. She also seemed very anxious about how she would get along with the other office staff since the only people she had met so far were the doctor and the main nurse. It should be pointed out that Selena was often very involved with her appearance and discussed clothing and her appearance a great deal.

Fortunately the group orientation for this group of interns was coming up and the coordinator made a point of discussing proper attire, and other interns were able to express some of the same concerns. The students were reminded that no one expected them to have a new wardrobe for their internships and that they would see when they got to the placement what others were wearing. As far as worrying about others in the workplace, the coordinator reminded them that this would be an ongoing issue throughout their lives—meeting and adjusting to new people that they may or may not feel comfortable with right away. The interns were reminded that they would have an orientation at the site during their first days and this would help them meet others and feel comfortable settling in. (As it turned out, Selena was given colorful scrubs to wear and instructed that dangling jewelry would not be very practical in a pediatrician's office.)

If students are beginning their internships at the same time, this stage can be addressed before they even get to their placements for the first time. Simply mentioning some of the characteristics of this stage will help students who don't know how to identify the feelings they are having. If students don't begin at the same time, it is a good idea to, individually or in small groups, talk about the issues that might be popping up in the initial stages of the internship experience.

Tips and Techniques

Stage One: Anticipation

- Start the intern on her journal before the placement actually starts. This way your student will be able to record some of her feelings about what she is looking forward to and any concerns.
- Conduct a group or individual orientation so that the intern knows "who is who" in the program and what to expect. This will also give the students a "heads up" on what is expected of them in dress, attendance, behaviors, and curriculum completion.
- Have a clear, structured curriculum, which is specific to the intern's placement site. This will then help the intern to focus on the learning that she will be gaining for the experience.
- Plan seminars that focus on learning, skill development, and give the students an opportunity to reflect and share their experiences and concerns.

STAGE TWO: EXPECTATIONS VS. REALITY

It is common for stage-two feelings to start shortly after the student has begun the internship. The intern begins to see the difference between what he expected or imagined and what the reality is. Here, the intern begins to shift from "what if" to "what is going wrong?" Feelings of frustration, anger, sadness, and disappointment may be felt. Sometimes an intern will direct these feelings toward the sponsor, the teacher/internship coordinator, customers, and his own self and abilities. If an intern begins to focus inward, he often begins to feel that good interns don't have these negative feelings or problems. Some interns describe feelings of frustration, anger, confusion, and sometimes panic at being in over their heads at this stage. A lot of new information needs to be processed at this stage, and some interns are overwhelmed by it all. An intern can easily begin to doubt his own competences and abilities.

If the feelings and behaviors expressed in this stage are not addressed, the intern may become stuck. Stage two is the stage when many internships fall apart.

During the first two weeks of his internship at a graphic arts company, James was very concerned that he would soon be expected to produce professional-level materials, as he had indicated during his interview that he "knew" many of the programs the company used, when in reality he had only a passing knowledge of most of them. His first week had been spent getting to know the other employees, spending time with them as they did their work, assisting verbally in some design concepts, and generally getting to know the company and the work they do. During the second week he was given some tasks to complete using the computer design programs used by most of the employees in the company. During the second advisory, he was very quiet (not in character for him).

Rather than ask directly what the problem was, the advisor asked the group to describe any examples of anxiety or fear of failure that the group might have. It took a while for the others to admit to experiencing situations where they felt like they might be in over their heads or situations in which they feared they would be required to do more than they felt they could. One student said she would feel like a "phony" if the sponsor asked her to do something she didn't feel able to do adequately. Further discussion enabled the students to see that all of them were having some of the same issues and that dealing with the problems calmly and directly was the adult way, not ignoring them and hoping they would clear up on their own.

In another instance of Stage Two: Expectations vs. Reality, we see problems with Caryn. The sponsor called the internship coordinator about Caryn's increasing tardiness and attitude shift. It seemed that she had begun to display a negative attitude when asked to attend staff meetings and assist staff members other than her immediate sponsor at a small animal clinic. She also seemed to be taking more breaks than necessary. The sponsor tried to talk with her about these issues, but Caryn stated that she didn't see a problem. She was doing her job. Other people took breaks. She was supposed to be learning from her sponsor and not the vet techs in the practice.

This situation required a private conversation with Caryn and then with both Caryn and the sponsor. It seemed that Caryn was working through her Internship Learning Plan (ILP) to the letter and couldn't understand why she needed to do other tasks even though they might expand her learning. She had no respect for the vet techs she was assigned to work with because she viewed them as "on her level" and not capable of teaching her anything. She was angry that the head veterinarian (sponsor) wasn't spending all of his time with her. In addition, she thought she was going to get to interact with the animals most of the time. This was clearly a case of confused expectations

At the next seminar, Caryn was asked to present her situation to the group, and afterward several students admitted that they were having similar issues. The group discussed ways to handle things both with suggestions from experience and brainstorming. All of the students were relieved to learn that they weren't the only ones to have these feelings. Several described feeling like "loser interns" for not being "up" about going to their placements. It took several more discussions, individual and group, to sort out all that was going on during this period.

Once the students recognized that they were going through a normal process and that they could become stuck here if they didn't address the problems, they seemed more willing to work on what they had to do to resolve the issues.

Recognizing that this stage can often make or break an internship experience is crucial. It is during this stage that an internship can fall apart. Each student reaches this point at a different time, but *usually* around the third to fifth week of an internship that students attend at least two times a week or the middle of the second month of a semester-long internship.

The excitement and newness have worn off. Some interns begin to feel disappointment that things are becoming routine and not quite what they expected, although it is difficult to get from them exactly what they expected. It is rare for a student not to go through some aspect of this stage. Some get bogged down and begin to find it hard to get themselves to the internship on time, start grumbling to friends and even adults that the internship is not what they expected. They also begin to question what is wrong and to think that what *they* are doing and feeling is wrong. Sometimes they blame the adults in the program—sponsors, internship coordinator, coworkers—for their feelings of disappointment, discouragement, and sometimes anger. Or they blame themselves.

Tips and Techniques

Stage Two: Expectation vs. Reality

- Encourage interns to use their journal entries to describe what is happening and their feelings.
- Use seminars to help students share their thoughts and feelings about how reality might not meet their expectations and help them see that this is part of the normal process.
- Help the students to see what they can do to improve their situation by encouraging them to problem solve issues themselves.
- Brief any mentor who might be involved with the students so that he or she can help the students to use their own problem solving skills.

STAGE THREE: FACING THE ISSUES

It is in this stage of the intern's placement that she begins to understand and deal with the issues, feelings, and behaviors that happened in stage two. Here the intern needs to talk about what has been happening and find a way to deal with the issues. Many of the issues here have to do with criticism and authority. Often the intern does not like being told what to do and may react in an unhelpful manner. This reaction to adult authority may be a pattern in the intern's life and is intensified by the experience in the workplace.

Once students have been helped to identify what is causing problems at the previous stage, they need to address these issues and problems. Some students need more help than others to clarify issues. This may be something they never thought of doing. Sometimes it is just a matter of adjusting the ILP and reviewing expectations. Sometimes it is more involved and requires several seminar sessions or individual discussions during site visits with the internship coordinator and/or sponsor.

In dealing with problems from stage two, students need help in identifying the actual problems. It may well be that the student has always had problems with authority, or perceived criticism, or sticking to routines, or taking direction. Young adults have very little experience in identifying their own feelings or their part in problems. They don't know how to "name" problems like adults do. Young adults aren't usually familiar with phrases such as "interpersonal issues," "team player," "unrealistic expectations," and so on. Many of them do not know how to resolve issues other than by fighting, using harsh words, or sticking their head in the sand. They just know they are uncomfortable and things are not going as they thought they should and they have no idea what to do about it. Now is the time for the adults in the program to play an active role.

Returning to James, after discussions about the various situations and possibilities of feelings and experiences that might crop up during this period, the students were able to write about this aspect of their internship in their journals. They were reminded that each of them had an ILP to guide what they were supposed to be doing and learning at the site and that they should feel free to discuss assignments (both those included in the ILP and those in addition to it) with the sponsor and internship coordinator.

It was pointed out that the sponsor agreed to have interns, to teach them and help them gain real-world experience, and certainly was not there to make them feel stupid or inadequate. If they felt that they didn't have enough experience or knowledge to complete a task, they should speak up. Just the experience of talking and writing about this stage helped most of the students. Several required private conversations.

James now felt he could approach the sponsor and ask if there were tutorials or manuals available for several of the programs he felt he needed to learn in detail. He did this, and soon was able to work through the tutorials both at his internship and at home. He also felt more comfortable asking coworkers questions without "feeling stupid."

As for Caryn, we can see that her issues required direct support from her internship coordinator, in addition to the support of her peers during advisory sessions. The internship coordinator and sponsor spoke in private on the phone and then the internship coordinator spoke with Caryn, explaining that although the ILP was the guide to the internship, it did not include all of the activities and tasks she was to do. This would be decided on a day-to-day basis depending on the needs of the clinic. In the meeting with Caryn and the sponsor, the internship coordinator acted as a support person for Caryn to explain her feelings and disappointments.

The sponsor listened carefully and recommended that Caryn talk with the vet techs about their training and requirements for their jobs so that she could see that they had training beyond "on the job" and that they were the backbone of the clinic. He also recommended that she visit a local college that offered a vet tech degree. Because she wanted more contact with the animals, the sponsor arranged for her to participate in prepping animals for surgery, and made sure to include her in every exam he performed, teaching her how to hold the animals during the exam. (Previously, the vet tech had only permitted her to observe.) He also made sure that she felt the door was open for her to come to him if she felt that she needed more responsibility.

At this point, Caryn expressed concern that she might accidentally hurt one of the animals and the sponsor reassured her that this was why she was assigned to work alongside the tech and himself. They would make sure that didn't happen, so she was able to relax and enjoy the placement more.

Tips and Techniques

Stage Three: Facing the Issues

- Facilitate group discussions in seminars about attitudes and behaviors when faced with criticism or authority.
- Encourage interns to use their journal entries to describe what is happening and their feelings.
- Brief any mentor who might be working with the student so that he can open discussions about the student's view of authority and behavior when faced with criticism.

STAGE FOUR: ACCOMPLISHMENT AND INDEPENDENCE

Dealing with and resolving the issues, feelings, and behaviors expressed in stage three helps the intern to move toward independence, confidence, effectiveness, and the ability to overcome obstacles. In this stage, which typically begins when the intern is feeling good about her skills, morale is high. The intern is moving toward autonomy as she is beginning to have success at tasks and assignments. At this stage, an intern will often ask for more challenging assignments from the supervisor, and for more time and attention from the supervisor and the teacher/coordinator. Sometimes the intern will need to find ways to juggle conflicting demands in her life.

After the conflicts and issues of stages two and three have been resolved (they will resurface periodically as some students need several attempts at resolving conflicts and readjusting their expectations of themselves and the internship as a whole before they can completely move on), students begin to really settle into their internship placement. This usually occurs toward the middle of the internship. However, each student is different and expecting everyone to arrive at a certain stage at the same time is unrealistic. The intern is feeling much better after having gotten through a very wobbly period. She is having greater success at the internship. Tasks are becoming more difficult and the intern can handle them. A great deal of the ILP has been completed. The intern begins to behave in a more professional manner and seems more sophisticated in the discussions of internship experiences during seminars.

However, there are problems associated with this stage that some interns, but not all, experience.

In his internship with a very large computer technology company, Rafael was able to accomplish a great deal and he seemed to be moving along just fine. About three-quarters of the way through the internship period, he began to complain, first to the internship coordinator and then to the group during seminar, that he felt he had learned "all there was to learn" at his placement and wondered why he could not be "promoted" to work with the CEO. More discussion revealed that Rafael had, indeed, completed his ILP (although it needed some more work in several areas); although he was involved in several interesting projects at the company, he felt he needed a position of "more importance." To his credit, he had the sense to not present his feelings in these words to his sponsor.

The internship coordinator, during a visit, learned that although Rafael was involved in projects that he had been describing in seminars and his journal as "interesting and okay," the role he was playing on the team was not much more than a supportive one.

However, he did have one assignment that required quite a bit of independent work, yet he did not focus on that task. Careful questioning revealed that in addition to wanting to "work with the CEO in an important place," he also felt he might, at this point, be leading his own team, not merely participating in its work as a team member. Rather than let him go on like this and sour his progress up to this point, the internship coordinator talked with him privately about the natural progression of job positions, how people gain positions of authority and power, and how he might handle his need to be seen as "important." For that was really the crux of the problem, in addition to not really knowing how businesses work in the real world.

A meeting with the sponsor, with the internship coordinator in a supporting role, enabled Rafael to explain that he wanted more responsibility and recognition for his part in the team's work. The sponsor helped him talk with the team leader who was under the impression that they were not supposed to "overwork the intern." She was very eager to give him more substantial tasks in the future. The sponsor also pointed out that the independent work that Rafael was to be doing on his own was very important to the department and would be presented as a section of a proposal to the CEO eventually. Rafael had not understood this at all.

Since Rafael still had his eye on the CEO's chair, the sponsor agreed to help him arrange an interview with him to allow him to ask, in addition to his other questions, how one got to the position of CEO of a major company and specifically how he *got to that position.*

In the next seminar, Rafael reported that he was feeling better, if not a little "overworked," but that was better than not feeling needed and important. He was able to explain to the group how he had talked with his sponsor and the team leader and was looking forward to his scheduled interview with the CEO the next week.

Another example deals with what can happen when a student has too many things to juggle.

At Ken's internship with a community newspaper, he was being given more and more assignments and was receiving quite a few compliments on his articles about local sports events. His family and peers remarked favorably to him when his articles appeared in the paper. However, Ken was getting frustrated at being responsible for covering all of the school's basketball home and away games for the paper. He felt overwhelmed that he was being asked to cover and write about all of the games and had no time to himself to enjoy sports with his friends. He also had to keep up with his other schoolwork and help out with his young sister after school some afternoons. Plus, he had most of his ILP left to do. The home games weren't so bad, but the away games took the entire late afternoon and evening.

Because he was so good at his job, the editor asked him to cover additional sports events in the community. One was an ice skating competition that ran into the weekend that he was planning to go away with his family to look at colleges. Ken expressed his building frustration and feelings of being overwhelmed at an advisory and also to the internship coordinator during a visit. Even though he was proud of his work and responsibility, he felt he was just overloaded and wasn't quite sure what to do about it. Ken didn't know how to say "no" professionally. And he needed help in prioritizing tasks and time management.

Luckily, a seminar session during that period dealt with time management and Ken (and the other students who were also feeling overwhelmed by everything in their lives) had very lively discussions about problems in this area and what to do about them. None of them had ever thought of this as a real issue that could be discussed and addressed. They weren't even familiar with the term "time management."

With the help of other interns, who were pretty sophisticated in their suggestions, Ken was able to schedule a meeting with his sponsor, calmly explain what was going on, and ask her how they could work together on the problem. The sponsor hadn't realized that she was "overloading" him, mainly because he seemed so cheerful about taking all assignments. Once she learned what he had on his plate, she made adjustments to what he was expected to do, and even assigned an employee to work with Ken for a few games so that she could take over some of the activities Ken was scheduled to cover, including the ice skating competition.

Although this stage may seem less problematic than the others, it is important to point out that an increasing commitment to work (at an internship) may place pressure on other aspects of life such as relationships or additional academic pursuits, and that students need to keep an eye out for time management issues and other personal challenges.

Tips and Techniques

Stage Four: Accomplishment and Independence

- Encourage interns to use their journal entries to record their accomplishments.
- In seminars probe accomplishments to make sure they are not superficial or too burdensome.
- Use seminars to explore careers and career paths as most students now feel confident about their abilities.
- In seminars focus specifically on:
    Time management
    Saying "no" professionally
    Setting priorities
    Setting objectives
- Brief mentors so that they are able to support the learning at this stage.

STAGE FIVE: CULMINATION

At this stage, the final one of the internship, the intern will show pride in what he has accomplished. But, at the same time, the intern could easily express sadness that the experience is ending. Often an intern might avoid facing these feelings of sadness and separation in avoidance behaviors such as joking, lateness, absence, and devaluing the experience.

One would think that this would be the easiest part of the internship experience, but that is not so. Although interns are nearing the end of their experience and are very proud of what they have achieved, many of them (probably most) have very specific problems with endings. Some can't leave or end anything without slamming a door. Others pull in and avoid their feelings. Some interns decide that the best way to deal with their confusing feelings is to joke around and pretend that none of it mattered anyway. *All* interns need a safe place to talk about what is going on and how they feel about it. They also need someone to talk to about how to handle these confusing feelings. It is during this stage that some interns nearly (or actually) destroy what they have accomplished by their inability to end an important activity or experience gracefully and with understanding.

If we do not help interns address this stage and permit some of them to "shoot themselves in the foot," we send the message that their selected behavior is the way to handle endings. This will cause them great problems throughout their lives.

Michelle began to come to her internship late during the last two to three weeks. She was also absent without calling ahead, which was totally out of character for her. The concerned sponsor called the school to discuss the matter. In the conversation she revealed that Michelle was beginning to "goof off" in the office, standing around chatting with other workers, wasting time at the mailboxes, and generally not completing her tasks. She was also not paying attention at staff meetings or team meetings and seemed to be doodling rather than taking notes and trying to understand what she was to be doing. As her team was in charge of getting a design plan out the door in less than a week, they really needed her input and contribution.

The sponsor needed help in understanding what was going on with her intern. A conversation about how interns often deal with separation and termination and the ending of an internship helped her to understand that Michelle was pretty much on track with her behavior. The problem was what to do about it as the project still had to be completed.

The sponsor agreed to have a private talk with Michelle, calmly noting the behavior and explaining why this was not acceptable. She also was to focus on how much Michelle's contribution meant to all at the small company. Then the sponsor scheduled an exit interview with Michelle so that there was a firm date on which they would discuss her performance. Michelle did not realize that this would be part of her internship and she sat up a bit straighter.

The sponsor also let Michelle know that she would be attending the presentations at the school later in the semester, and she was looking forward to Michelle's presentation and offered to help her prepare it, even though the internship would have ended by then. In addition, the office was planning a farewell breakfast on the last day of Michelle's time there, which both surprised and pleased her. She needed to know that her presence mattered and that people would miss her.

At the next to last advisory, Michelle was proud to tell the group about the "professional exit interview" she would be having and the office get-together that was planned. She was able to join the others in discussing her feelings about ending what was a very good experience for her.

Tips and Techniques

Stage Five: Culmination

- Review the sponsor evaluation of the intern, focusing on both accomplishments and areas for further development.
- Review the student's evaluation of his experience and focus on the future.
- Do an individual learning or development plan with the student so that he can take his learning forward.
- Use the seminar to help the student understand some of the feelings he may be having at the end of his experience.
- Use the seminar to celebrate accomplishments.
- Use the student portfolio to help the student see all that he has learned and how to use the learning and new skills in the next phase of his life.
- Use the presentation or exhibit as a way for the student to gain recognition from others for his work.
- Brief mentors and encourage them to talk about "endings," accomplishments, and moving forward.

Internships can give students the real-world experience that is critical for building the skills and behaviors they will need in their careers or further education. However, young people often need guidance and support as they move into unfamiliar places with new people. Understanding the behaviors some students exhibit and taking positive actions will help coordinators and sponsors guide and support them as they continue to learn and develop. Helping students to navigate the world of work under the guidance of the school will help to ensure their future success.

NOTES

1. Joel F. Diambra, Kylie G. Cole-Zakrzewski, and Josh Booher, "A Comparison of Internship Stage Models: Evidence from Intern Experiences," *Journal of Experiential Education* 27, no. 2 (2004): 210.

2. H. Frederick Sweitzer and Mary A. King, *The Successful Internship: Personal, Professional, and Civic Development* (Belmont, CA: Brooks/Cole, 2009).

3. Robert P. Inkster and Roseanna Gaye Ross, *The Internship as Partnership: A Handbook for Campus-Based Coordinators and Advisors* (Raleigh, NC: National Society for Experiential Education, 1995).

4. Pamela Myers Kiser, *The Human Services Internship: Getting the Most from Your Experience*, 3rd ed. (Independence, KY: Brooks/Cole, Cengage Learning, 2012).

Chapter Nine

The Power of Internships

Real Schools, Real Stories

> If I had an internship when I was in high school, it wouldn't have taken me so long to figure out what I wanted to do.

> —Internship Sponsor

Like the sponsor quoted above, practically everyone expresses enthusiasm for internships, not only wishing they had had an opportunity for the experience, but also supporting the idea that all young adults should have a chance to try out learning in the real world. When asked why internships weren't part of their education, most people respond that their schools didn't—or don't—offer them. Although increasing numbers of schools are adding internships to their curriculum, the vast majority of secondary schools have not done so for a variety of reasons: finances, programmatic issues, perceived lack of internship sites, and general lack of administrative or staff support.

This chapter sets out to show where and how internships can be interwoven into any high school program, in any community. It draws from experience with a variety of programs in many different settings where internships have worked and also discusses settings in which internships would be an asset to the school's course offerings or curriculum.

STORIES FROM THE FIELD: THE POWER OF INTERNSHIPS

Throughout our years working with individual schools and districts, we have seen internship programs used and adapted for almost every type of school program in schools of varying size, in practically every type of location.

In all of the possible settings for internships, the one thread running through them all is that of relationships. Chapter 4 discussed the importance of relationships between the three main players in the monitoring of the internship experience. But beyond the regular day-to-day contact and interactions, internships can be much more—they can foster positive relationships with adults for students who might never have felt connected to the school or adults in general.

For those who have turned their backs on education and now need a face-saving way back in, relationships with other students in the same boat and the adults who are helping them can make a world of difference. Those who have had no positive or special experiences during their entire school career begin to see that the growing relationships with peers, teachers, and sponsors have given them the ability to shine at their internship and present their work with a self-assuredness that surprises everyone.

And even the "stars"—those who have made their journey through school collecting praise and awards, the highest grades, and wide recognition—are challenged when they meet experts in the world of work who are willing to act as their sponsors while they are asked to put their school achievements to work in the real world where no one knows how many As are on their report cards or trophies on the mantel.

The following examples and vignettes show not only how the inclusion of quality internship programs can enrich a school's educational opportunities but also the importance of the interpersonal relationships in each setting.

ALTERNATIVE EDUCATION, DROPOUT PREVENTION AND RETRIEVAL, CREDIT RECOVERY, SCHOOLS FOR AT-RISK YOUTH

It is difficult to totally separate programs designed to address the needs of students designated as at risk, or dropouts, or those in need of alternative educational settings. There is no pure model, as aspects of one include aspects of the others. It is, however, possible to state that whatever the focus of the school is, internships benefit the students and add an element usually absent in their former schools—real-world learning.

In his TED Talk "How to Escape Education's Death Valley," Sir Ken Robinson remarked:

> Every student who drops out of school has a reason for it, which is rooted in their own biography. They may find it boring. They may find it irrelevant. They may find that it's at odds with the life they're living outside of school. There are trends, but the stories are always unique. I was at a meeting recently in Los Angeles of—they're called alternative education programs. These are programs designed to get kids back into education. They have certain common features. They're very personalized. They have strong support for the teachers, close links with the community, and a broad and diverse curriculum, and often programs which involve students outside school as well as inside school. And they work. What's interesting to me is these are called "alternative education.". . . And all the evidence from around the world is if we all did that, there'd be no need for the alternative.[1]

If this clip were shown to most of the interns we have encountered, there would be a very loud cheer going up, for internships are indeed an alternative—an alternative to sitting in a classroom all day, staring at the back of someone else's head or staring out the window.

Luckily some public schools and districts realize that among their various school offerings there should be a program for students who are not successful in a large public school. These alternative programs offer students smaller classes, more direct instruction, and an environment where the individual student "matters" and individual relationships can be nurtured. Self-motivated students can usually thrive anywhere, but alternative high schools suit those who need a bit of extra assistance and instruction to succeed. Many special education students and English language learners also benefit greatly from the smaller classes and more relationship-driven classes and real-world experiences of alternative programs.

One exemplary alternative high school serving a unique student population in New York City has been doing so for over forty years—through a robust program of internships. This school, because of its location in a large city, is able to offer its students the option of interning at several sites simultaneously, combining experiential learning with in-house classes meant to supplement the learning gained at the internships. The population of the student body ranges from students who have tired of the stress of competitive "special" academic high schools, to those who have become bored at their local schools and are on the verge of dropping out, to those who have already dropped out and have missed so much school that they feel they may never catch up, to those who are homeless and living in nearby squats with other students who realize that without a high school diploma there is no future for them. And alongside these at-risk students are professional working young adults who are often on the road, students who want to accelerate their graduation, and those who simply want to try out learning in the real world.

Throughout the years, students at this school have been able to form meaningful relationships with not only the teachers on staff, but with multiple sponsors of the internships they were able to experience. One student who had been suspended from several other high schools was able to find success at a four-star restaurant. After other experiences in three- and four-star restaurants, he attended a culinary school and eventually became a chef at a well-known restaurant. Another student, who left a stressful situation in a school for the gifted, interned with several photographers, completed her high school diploma, and was admitted to a college honors program in photography.

Another alternative program in a suburban community, designed as a dropout retrieval program, used internships as a way to entice the students to spend half a day in the building, making up lost credits and sending them out into the community for structured internships four afternoons a week, with one afternoon reserved for seminars and group/class activities. This type of program seemed to work well for the students who were not too keen on being in the building at all. As one of the teachers remarked, "Why would they come back to the same thing that caused them to drop out in the first place?" These students were willing to do the work necessary for credit recovery because they were able to leave the building and do something they elected to do.

> *Why would they come back to the same thing that caused them to drop out in the first place?*
> *—Alternative School Teacher*

In another type of alternative school, a continuation high school, internships have been added to the offerings and have proved to be extremely popular with the students, even though most of them are juggling paid work, families, and making up lost school credits.

The goal of continuation high schools is to increase the chances for vulnerable, at-risk students to complete their education while better preparing them for employment and self-sufficiency. In these schools, students often form very close relationships with staff and rarely slip through the cracks as often happens at larger comprehensive schools. A unique feature of continuation high schools is the variety of programs offered to students. Such programs include career orientation and counseling, work-study assistance, job placement, and internships.

Experience with one continuation high school in California revealed that of all the programmatic support, flexibility, and individualization available, the students valued their internship experiences the most—even those who already had jobs were eager to pursue an internship because they did not view their paying jobs to be the source of a career path. Students who had not previously thought beyond simply getting their diplomas were encouraged by their teachers to give thought to options, try out possible careers, and think beyond limited horizons. Many students needed to rely on their relationships with school staff to arrange complicated schedules, childcare, and transportation (one young man rode the bus to school, picked up a bicycle he kept there and rode to his internship placement). But his success and experience at his internships made the effort worthwhile.

A Real Alternative

As surprising it may seem, internships have proven to be successful in a school for court-remanded youth. In one small rural high school in a mid-Atlantic state, the staff decided that the students who were remanded to the facility and attended the school there needed more than just classroom experience. With strong leadership and determination, they developed and piloted an internship program for students who had been selected based on their work, behavior, and other criteria designed to ensure the success of the program. Finding sponsors in the local community was not the challenge the staff thought it would be. Placements were found for interns with a veterinarian, several different departments in a hospital, a senior center, and a community newspaper. Transportation was the main challenge, but using the school's driver's education car and a combination of buses and cars solved that.

Had the superintendent and principal not been strong supporters, the program would not have succeeded—but they were, and the program grew. Students who were not selected soon became keenly interested in learning what they could do to improve their chances to be chosen to participate. Students who were scheduled to return to their home communities found themselves not wanting to leave. Many wrote back, expressing that the internship had been the most important thing in their lives. The staff at the school and the sponsors had been the only adults who had taken time to teach and help them, and they were glad someone had pointed them in a different direction from what had brought them to the school in the first place.

Career and Technical Education Programs

Unlike a traditional high school that focuses only on academics, vocational schools (which exist in various forms and might be called career and technical eduation [CTEs], career academies, area CTE schools, vocational technical schools, trade schools, or other variations) offer a blend of academics and hands-on training to prepare graduates for careers in fields as varied as nursing, marketing, auto repair, fashion design, architecture, computer science, agricultural science, aircraft mechanics, hospitality management, plumbing, manufacturing, protective services, and library science, to name a few. In many instances, students attend their local secondary school for part of the day and the CTE school for the other part.

Hands-on experience is an integral part of CTE, and most programs have stringent curriculum and requirements. Some career areas, however, do lend themselves to a more flexible, experiential learning experience in the form of an internship.

One CTE school in a mid-Atlantic state undertook to expand its work-based learning experiences for its students by updating the curriculum that guided the experiences, finding time for teachers to visit students in the field, instituting a class that would pull all students in to discuss their work-based experiences and work on other career-related activities, and prepare the students for end-of-year presentations, something that had never been tried before. Needless to say, all of the changes did not occur at once, but gradually the staff and students adapted to the changes and reported that their program had become richer since the changes have taken place.

During a visit to the program, observers saw that a student in an emergency responder program who at first had been having difficulty settling into the program did not realize that a call coming over the radio meant that he was to suit up and go with the fire department EMS team to a real, not simulated, emergency. The look on his face was priceless as he prepared for his first foray into the real world of EMS work. After he returned to the school, his whole attitude changed and his class work was exemplary. His comment to the teacher was that the EMS team needed his help and he didn't have time to just observe—he had to work and that was fine by him. He sat near the radio for the rest of the term, eager for the call that would mean he was "on deck."

Senior Projects

Senior projects have been in use by high schools for many years; most include four elements—paper, project, portfolio, and presentation. In addition to a qualitatively different experience that enables seniors to become intensely involved in an area of interest, senior projects give them greater control over their own learning and opportunities to reflect upon the meaning of their education. Seniors are able to develop relationships with teachers and other adults that encourage cooperative research and the exchange of ideas. In some schools, the senior project is used to combat senioritis, a condition usually emerging during the second semester of the senior year. Even if a school does not have a formal senior project program, internships have been used to combat this prevalent condition.

Whatever the purpose of implementing senior projects, in many programs the project segment takes the form of an internship.

Because the school needs to keep things going as the year progresses, implementing a senior project or senior internship program can be a lot like changing tires on a moving school bus. And often the internship part and the presentation are not as robust as they could be simply because of lack of resources—mainly time. When senior projects are given the resources they need, magical things happen with the students.

In observing many, many students of all ability levels as they present their projects and internship experiences at a New York State suburban countywide annual student exhibition conference over the past sixteen years, it has been apparent that there are immeasurable benefits to these types for programs for all students. And student comments during most of the presentations referred to the importance of the relationships that formed while the students were interning with local politicians, stockbrokers, airport control towers, top-notch restaurants, cultural institutions, specialized schools, homes for seniors, landscape designers—the list is very long and varied.

Some students have changed their plans for majors in college based on internship experiences. Some have gotten full scholarships as a result of second college interviews in which they described their independent work at an internship. Some have formed relationships with their sponsors that have lasted through college and beyond. Some have a mentor for life and some have even secured jobs after graduation. All of the students have a different view of adults and the world of work after spending time in the world outside of the schoolhouse walls.

The coordinators of these programs report that their students grow immensely in the time spent in the internships. Small tips from sponsors and colleagues on how to shake hands confidently become a big learning experience when students realize this will benefit them for the rest of their working lives. Instructions on how to not call negative attention to oneself at a client or board meeting, with rows of earrings and facial piercings (take them off!) goes down better when delivered by a sponsor than a parent or teacher. Students who would never have completed a project are able to do so with the guidance of a sponsor and are able to present their accomplishments to an audience of strangers because they have been explaining their project to new people in the workplace all along—and their sponsor is in the audience, along with their grandmother.

Service Learning

Service learning is a method of teaching, learning, and reflecting that combines academic classroom curriculum with meaningful service throughout the community. As a teaching methodology, it falls under the category of experiential education. More specifically, it integrates meaningful community service with instruction and reflection to enrich the learning experience, teach civic responsibility, encourage lifelong civic engagement, and strengthen communities for the common good.

Service learning should not be confused with mandated community service hours required for graduation or as a form of punishment.

The elements of quality internships can also apply to service learning placements. The sites may have a different focus—that of performing a project of benefit to the community—but the principles are the same. Students need to have guidance in their activities, and the organizations that host them need to understand that they are not just serving, but learning.

Small Learning Communities (Schools-within-Schools)

Small learning communities (SLCs) can take several forms. One of the primary models, which includes internships, is the career academy program. In other SLCs, themed houses serve as the SLCs. This was the case in one high school in a small city in New England that wanted to address several problems at once and formed an "academy" around the theme of work-based learning. Students very quickly embraced the idea of "getting out of school" and, even after realizing that this would most likely require even more work than they had been complaining about, settled down and did very well at their internship placements. Being out of the building also kept them from the negative encounters that had been the story of their school careers. They were too busy to get into arguments about who bumped into whom and certainly did not see that type of behavior being modeled at their internship placements.

Feedback from the sponsors of the interns ranged from "We recommend that Jane receive full credit for her internship. She is a delightful woman who is eager to work, quick to learn, and is an asset to our organization" to "Michael has done exceptional work at XYZ Planners. His responsibilities increased weekly and he excelled in all areas" to "Everyone at our office will miss Carol's presence. She has been an integral part of our design team and has contributed a unique and vital perspective to projects."

Night High Schools

We know from colleagues that internships work well in comprehensive night high schools with students who are working for pay during regular business hours and study for a high school diploma in the evenings. Many of them welcome a chance to try out new careers as post-graduation options, and sponsors welcome them because they are mature and have work experience.

Other Schools That Could Benefit from Internships

In addition to the school models and programs discussed here, there are many more schools that are a good fit for an internship program. Some of these schools already have an internship component tucked into various programs or departments and could expand the programs to include more students.

Because of their flexibility, charter schools, home schools, and independent study programs would be ideal for providing internship opportunities for their students. Summer schools, year-round schools, and extended-day programs are ideal homes for internship programs because of their ability to have flexibility in their scheduling. Many middle college high schools, early college high schools, and STEM academies are connected with college campuses and area businesses and provide, or could provide, internship opportunities for their students. Increasingly community colleges afford time for students to integrate interships into their regular academic programs.

Although the focus of a school's internship structure and philosophy may differ, the basic quality principles remain the same. Quality internships are quality internships. And students benefit if internships are done well.

NOTE

1. Kenneth Robinson, "How to Escape Education's Death Valley," TED Talks: Education, 19:11. May 2013. www.ted.com/talks/ken_robinson_how_to_escape_education_s_death_valley.html.

Afterword

We've written this book because of our belief that internships give students the real-world experience that is critical for building the skills and behaviors they will need in their careers and further education. This belief is shared by many of our colleagues across the country—teachers and administrators who have been determined to develop programs that afford their students the opportunity to experience an internship. When we have worked and talked with them we learned that not only are students affected by their internships, teachers have been reenergized by becoming coordinators or adding an internship component to their classes.

Teachers who were burned out and about to leave teaching have found new inspiration for their professional careers. Some educators who have been involved with internship programs for several years remarked that their experiences with interns have provided wonderful memories—stories from former interns who have kept in touch with coordinators, sponsors, and schools, and report success that they attribute to their life-changing internship experience.

The thread that runs through each colleague's story focuses on the positive feedback from all: from students who changed their minds and majors to students who could remember their internship experiences vividly, after five, ten, even fifteen years; from sponsors who had started out as interns and now were helping high school students the way they had been helped to sponsors who wondered why all high schools didn't have internship programs for all adolescents.

Developing a quality internships program takes time and commitment, but as educators we owe it to our students to make sure they have the opportunity to develop skills needed for the new economy and to grow personally and socially before they move into their next stage of life. Internships are a challenge, but doable—not impossible. Schools have risen to the challenge and their students have benefited greatly. With some determination and support it can be done.

There are challenges, but because many schools have gone through the development process, some of the challenges can be reduced, but not totally eliminated. Schools will still have to address issues such as schedule adjustments, staff programming, transportation, and liability. But determined schools have found these issue are not insurmountable.

An internship program can be developed and implemented within a reasonable amount of time. Budgets, although tight and getting tighter, *can* be adjusted with flexibility in scheduling and allotment of resources. We have not suggested using grants to operate internship programs. In our experience we have found that schools that begin internship programs on soft money (grants) often lose those programs when the grant period ends because the program was considered an add-on to the regular school structure, and no allowance was made for sustainability. Although some schools have begun programs on grant money, they have sustained their programs through incorporation of internships into the culture and program of the school.

As principals of Internship Quest, LLC, we have had numerous conversations with administrators, teachers, and principals about setting up internship programs. Principals are concerned that in this time of limited resources and emphasis on testing, programs needs be easily managed and show outcomes. Teachers are concerned that they do not have the time to invest in developing a program. The common comment is that no one has time to reinvent the wheel.

As one writer noted in an article about internships for adolescents, "New and existing programs would benefit from improved access to field-tested program materials, detailed implementation guidelines, research on effective practices and professional development opportunities with internship program veterans."[1] We want this book to provide some of those implementation guidelines and effective practices.

Internship Quest (www.internshipquest.com) supports internship development with its materials, and some states have guides for career internship materials on their websites. Colleagues in the field want to get a jump-start on all the paperwork required. This is what they asked for; this is what they need.

We know that when pre-written Internship Learning Plans across career clusters, which can easily be tailored to a specific site or used as written, are used, schools find that starting a program is within their resources and timeframe. A prewritten handbook for students, which gives the guidelines for completing ILPs and specific uniform goals, helps the intern to easily organize work in one place, either in hardcopy or electronically.

Sponsors also tell us that materials that have been produced precisely for them makes them feel connected to the school and the program.

These types of materials ensure that the program can be sustained year after year as new ILPs are added and student and sponsor input helps to tailor their handbooks.

We know that starting an internship program can seem daunting but we also know that a good program excites and engages all students. And we know that students are asking to be challenged and engaged. They are eager to take the next steps to get out into the real world but they need us to believe in them and support them as they move into the next stage of their lives.

More and more educators are beginning to recognize the power internships have on student engagement and learning. We hope you believe, as we do, that quality internships can help shape the future of our young people. Going forward, in this day and age, internships are not just an interesting experience—they are a necessity for all students.

NOTE

1. Eliot Levine, "The Rigors and Rewards of Internships," *Educational Leadership* 68, no. 1 (September 2010): 48.

Appendix

1. Sample Internship Learning Plans
   a. Architecture Internship Learning Plan
   b. Veterinarian Internship Learning Plan
   c. Ecology Internship Learning Plan

2. Sample Liability Statements

3. USDOL Fact Sheet #71: Internship Programs under the Fair Labor Standards Act

Architectural Firm

Architectural Assistant

Description: The A and A Architectural Firm is a medium sized company that designs a variety of buildings from individual houses to large commercial spaces.

General Responsibilities: The Intern will be involved in basic architectural drafting, production work, model making, creation of scale models with a 3D printer and site inspection and analysis. There will also be involvement in client contact and meetings.

Goal #1   U n i f o r m Goals and Self Evaluation

Please complete the checked **Uniform Goals** by the date agreed upon. Detailed instructions for completing the Uniform Goals can be found in your *Student Handbook*

		Date Due
☐	**1. Journal**	
☐	**2. Literature in Field**	
☐	**3. Career Path Research**	
☐	**4. Vocabulary**	
☐	**5. Organizational Structure**	
☐	**6. Sponsor Interview**	
☐	**7. Entry for a Resume**	
☐	**8. Description for Transcript**	
☐	**9. Thank You Letter**	
☐	**10. Student Self Evaluation**	

In addition to the Uniform Goals, the following Goals and Activities are to be completed by the dates agreed upon:

Goal #2   To learn all office procedures

Activities: Observe and participate in all office activities including all phases of drawing, designs as well as assisting architects on their on-going projects.

Goal #3 To learn the basics of "presentation" drawings

Activities: Practice lettering, designing, blue line printing, model building and all other steps involved in producing the plans for a building project.

Goal #4 To learn the components and purpose of a site inspection

Activities: Visit several sites with the architects. Sketch several, noting the important features mentioned by the architects. Answer the following questions:
Why is a site visit necessary? How many visits are made to a site? What things are the architects looking for when the visit? How do they note their findings? How is this used in the drawings and design of the buildings?

Goal #5 To learn architectural drawing

Activities: Select and complete five drawings from the list below:

general drafting	reflected ceiling plans (a ceiling drawing)	Sketches template uses
tracing work	furniture details	Riser diagrams (show all plumbing fixtures)
plot plans (aerial view)	door and window	Bathroom details
foundation plans (" of structure)	seating arrangements	wall plans
sections (cut view of house) elevations (side view of house)	revisions on original	

Goal # 6 To become familiar with necessary vocabulary and terminology in this field

Activity: Create a glossary of technical terms, vocabulary and phrases and acronyms specific to this internship. In addition to defining the works and terms in this ILP, add any others that you learn during the course of the internship.

Barrier free designs	Grid paper	Plumbing, (mechanical, electrical, architectural, structural)
Blue Prints	Mylars	SPECS
CAD	3D Printing	Title blocks
Fenestration		Topography

Goal # 7 Develop a project such as a small building, a garage, shop or single- space building.

Activities: Follow the steps you have learned from your sponsors from concept to design to building a model and be prepared to write your procedures and exhibit your model.

Evaluation of Student Work: See Evaluation section in Student Handbook. Select an appropriate method from the evaluation activity list.

 **Internship Quest**

Veterinary Hospital

Veterinary Assistant

Description: The Veterinary Hospital provides full service health care for animals including testing, surgery and animal health maintenance.

General Responsibilities: The intern will participate in caring for animals. The intern needs to enjoy working with animals and be willing to learn.

Goal #1   Uniform Goals and Self Evaluation

Please complete the checked **Uniform Goals** by the date agreed upon. Detailed instructions for completing the Uniform Goals can be found on the instructions in your ***Student Handbook***.

	Date Due
☐ 1. Journal	
☐ 2. Literature in Field	
☐ 3. Career Path Research	
☐ 4. Vocabulary	
☐ 5. Organizational Structure	
☐ 6. Sponsor Interview	
☐ 7. Entry for a Resume	
☐ 8. Description for Transcript	
☐ 9. Thank You Letter	
☐ 10. Student Self Evaluation	

In addition to the Uniform Goals, the following Goals and Activities are to be completed by the dates agreed upon.

Goal #2 Learn veterinary procedures and carry out with supervision

Activities: Practice the following procedures:
- Giving liquid orally
- Giving tablets orally
- Calculating dosing of vaccines and lab medication
- Giving injections
- Assisting in surgery
- Performing lab tests
- Drawing blood sample
-

Goal #3 Learn the scope of activities performed in a veterinary practice
Activities:
- Process medical supplies; help keep animals cared for and animal area clean; prepare equipment and instruments for examinations and surgery.
- Keep a journal describing work done. Work under supervision of internship supervisor.
-

Goal # 4 Learn to perform lab tests
Activity: Choose two of the following: Heartworm, fecal parasites, ear mites, skin scrapings and perform tests under the supervision of internship supervisor.

Goal #5 Observe and assist the doctor in routine exams and surgical procedures
Activity:
Complete and submit 6 briefs of procedures to internship supervisor. (3 reports of exams and 3 reports of surgical procedures) Include the following:
- Proper way to pickup/ hold /restrain various animals for examination and treatment
- Species of animal, age, sex
- Reason for surgery
- Describe surgical procedure
- Post-surgery treatment and prognosis for recovery

Goal #6 Learn to identify 3 diseases or syndromes and three treatments prescribed. Study the available information and complete the questions.
Activity: Describe the prognosis with and without treatment.

DISEASE IDENTIFICATION FORM
Possible choices: Heartworm Infection, Feline Leukemia (FEIV), Feline Immunodeficiency Syndrome (FIV), Specific parasitic infections, (i.e.: skin, intestinal, etc.), Feline Urological Syndrome (FUS), Upper Respiratory Infection (URI), Parvovirus, Coronavirus, etc...

1. Identification of disease or syndrome
2. What animal species does the disease affect? (Age group, sex, if applicable)
3. How does the disease occur and how is it transmitted?
4. List the common symptoms of the disease or syndrome. Also list rare symptoms if applicable.
5. List the currently used treatment for the disease or syndrome. Also list preventatives if applicable.

Goal #7 *Learn the vocabulary specific to your internship Activity:*
Create a glossary of technical terms, vocabulary, phrases and acronyms specific to this internship. In addition to defining the words and terms listed here, add others that you learn during the course of your internship. This goal meets the requirements of Uniform Goal 4.

breeding	foundering
canine distemper	heartworms
colic	heat period
cribbing	hip dysplasia
declaw	kennel cough
distemper	lyme disease
euthanasia	neuter
feline leukemia	parvovirus
fleas	ticks

Evaluation of Student Work: See Evaluation section in *Student Handbook.* Select an appropriate method from the evaluation activity list.

Marshland Conservation Ecology Intern

This internship may be in local government conservation or natural resources department, a non-profit conservation project, a local environmental studies university department or a local Museum of Natural History. The intern will be applying science concepts and taking a critical look at challenges of preserving marshland for the future.

Description: Marshland Conservation is dedicated to the protection and restoration of Marshland and marshland wildlife through research, education, and hands-on programs in ecology.

General Responsibilities: This is an opportunity for the intern to learn about the marshland, how our ecosystem works, how the marshland habitat sustains the fish, birds and other animals of the region. It is also an opportunity for the intern to communicate to others the challenges facing marshland preservation. The intern will help administratively, do at least one research project, and lead tours of the facility.

This is an ideal internship for students who are interested in our environment, want to conserve wildlife habitat and/or who want to work outside.

Goal #1   Uniform Goals and Self Evaluation

Please complete the checked **Uniform Goals** by the date agreed upon. Detailed instructions for completing the Uniform Goals can be found on the instructions in your **Student Handbook**.

	Date Due
☐ **1. Journal**	
☐ **2. Literature in Field**	
☐ **3. Career Path Research**	
☐ **4. Vocabulary**	
☐ **5. Organizational Structure**	
☐ **6. Sponsor Interview**	
☐ **7. Entry for a Resume**	
☐ **8. Description for Transcript**	
☐ **9. Thank You Letter**	
☐ **10. Student Self Evaluation**	

In addition to the Uniform Goals, the following Goals and Activities are to be completed by the dates agreed upon.

Goal #2 U n d e r s t a n d the role of Marshland Conservation
Activities:
1. Interview the director of Conservation project or department and ask these questions:
- What makes up Marshland?
- What is happening to the marshland and why is that important?
- What kind of animals and/or fish lives in the Marshland?
- What needs to be done to preserve the marshlands?

2. Produce a short YouTube video (2-3 minutes) telling the story of why marshlands are important and what needs to be done to preserve them. Upload you video and track viewers and any feedback.

Goal #3 Participate in the day-to-day activities of the organization
Activities:
Participate in administrative and day-to-day activities as needed. These may include:
- maintaining a record of animals in the marshland
-monitoring and clearing obstructions in the marshland
-Talking to visitors to the project/department about the marshland work
-Assisting in tours of the marsh
-Assisting in preparation and delivery of "show and tell" about the marshland for elementary school children
Participating in public relations and community education events

Goal #4 Gain An Understanding Of The 24/7 Life Of The Marshland
Activities:
1. Monitor any webcam set up to watch animal and bird life
-List the animals and birds you saw?
-List the times the animals and birds were seen?
-What is the difference between the night and day life of the marsh?
-Maintain a log of animal and bird sightings including required observation notes

2.Write a blog about tracking the sightings of marshland animals and birds showing how often and when they visit the Marsh and post to website. Monitor and respond to any feedback.

Goal #5 Learn the essential concepts of ecology
Activities:
Using the Internet or local library define ecology.
Describe how marshland conservation is part of ecology.
Describe the ecological challenges facing marshland.
Write an informational brief suitable for a selected age group and include in your Portfolio.

Goal #6 Learn the vocabulary and terms specific to your internship
Activity:
Create a glossary of technical terms, vocabulary, phrases and acronyms specific to this internship. In addition to defining the words and terms listed here, add others that you learn during the course of your internship. This goal meets the requirements of Uniform Goal 4.

acid rain	ecology	PCBs
biodegradable	ecosystem	pollution
biosphere	environment	Salt water marshland
Biting fly control	Fresh water marshland	sediment
brackish	habitat	salinity
clear cutting	Impounded marsh	Wet land food chain
conservation	Invasive plant species	
cordgrass	Mosquito vector control	

Evaluation of Student Work: See Evaluation section in *Student Handbook.* Select an appropriate method from the evaluation activity list.

Samples of Liability Agreements

One New York State SCHOOL DISTRICT AGREEMENT

THIS AGREEMENT is made between the Central School District Superintendent of Schools, hereinafter called the **SUPERINTENDENT**

and_____

_____ hereinafter called the **INTERNSHIP SITE**.

WHEREAS, the **SUPERINTENDENT**, through the **COMMUNITY AS SCHOOL PROJECT**, hereinafter
called the **CAS PROJECT**, desires to provide instruction and training for students in the **CAS PROJECT**; and **WHEREAS**, the **INTERNSHIP SITE** is able to provide the external learning site and "real- life" type learning experiences for said course subject (s) to the terms and conditions as hereinafter set forth;

NOW, THEREFORE, the **SUPERINTENDENT** and the **INTERNSHIP SITE** agree as follows:

1. The **INTERNSHIP SITE** shall enter into an agreement with the **SUPERINTENDENT**, through the **CAS PROJECT**, to provide external learning experiences to students from the **CAS PROJECT**.

2. It is understood that these classes will be conducted on any of the seven days of the weeks during the____school term.

3. The students shall be subject to the rules and regulations of the **INTERNSHIP SITE'S** facilities. All students are under the discipline and authority of the staff of the **CAS PROJECT.**

4. The **INTERNSHIP SITE** agrees that the **CAS PROJECT** students shall not displace any regular employee of the **INTERNSHIP SITE** nor shall the student's training activities preclude the firing of additional employees.

5. The **SUPERINTENDENT** shall provide necessary compensation and liability insurance for bodily injury and property damage in the amount of $1,000,000.00 each while students are on the __premises of the **INTERNSHIP SITE** and shall hold harmless the **INTERNSHIP SITE**, its officers, agents, and employees from liability, loss, damage, or expenses which may be incurred in the operation of this agreement except for liability resulting from the sole negligence or willful misconduct, or independent contractors who are directly employed by the **INTERNSHIP SITE**; and the **INTERNSHIP SITE** shall be held harmless for any injury to or death of persons or damage to property caused by an act, neglect, default, or omission of the **SUPERINTENDENT**, its employees, or students.

IN WITNESS WHEREOF, the parties hereto have executed this **AGREEMENT**.

Dated:_____By:_____

Beatrice James, Superintendent

Agreement

THIS AGREEMENT is made between the County Superintendent of Schools hereinafter, called the **SUPERINTENDENT**, and_____
hereinafter called the **INTERNSHIP SITE**.

WHEREAS, the **SUPERINTENDENT**, through the **COMMUNITY AS SCHOOL** program, desires to provide instruction and training for students in the **COMMUNITY ALLIANCE PROGRAM**; and

WHEREAS, the **INTERNSHIP SITE** is able to provide the external learning site and "real-life" type learning experiences for said course subject to the terms and conditions as hereinafter set forth;

NOW, THEREFORE, the **SUPERINTENDENT** and the **INTERNSHIP SITE** agree as follows:

1. The **INTERNSHIP SITE** shall enter into an agreement with the **SUPERINTENDENT**, through the **COMMUNITY AS SCHOOL** program, to provide external learning experiences to students from **COMMUNITY ALLIANCE PROGRAM**.
2. It is understood that these classes will be conducted on any of the seven days of the week during the 20-------- school term.
3. The students shall be subject to the rules and regulations of the **INTERNSHIP SITE** during the hours they are in the **INTERNSHIP SITE'S** facilities. All students are under the discipline and authority of the staff of **COMMUNITY ALLIANCE PROGRAM**.
4. The **INTERNSHIP SITE** agrees that the **COMMUNITY AS SCHOOL** students shall not displace any regular employee of the **INTERNSHIP SITE** not shall the student's training activities preclude the firing of additional employees.
5. The **SUPERINTENDENT** shall provide necessary compensation and liability insurance of bodily injury and property damage in the amount of $5,000,000.00 each while the students are on the premises of the **INTERNSHIP SITE** and shall hold harmless the **INTERNSHIP SITE**, its officers, agents, and employees from liability, loss, damage, or expenses which may be incurred in the operation of this agreement except for liability resulting from the sole negligence or willful misconduct of the **INTERNSHIP SITE**, its officers, employees, agents, or independent contractors who are directly employed by the **INTERNSHIP SITE**; and the **INTERNSHIP SITE** shall be held harmless for any injury to or death of persons or damage to property caused by an act, neglect, default, or omission of the superintendent, its employees, or students.

IN WITNESS WHEREOF, the parties hereto have executed this **AGREEMENT**.

Dated _____   _____
                                                    Tom Smith, Superintendent of Schools
Dated _____   _____
                                    Robert Jones, Assistant Superintendent of Business Services
Dated _____   _____
                                                    Jane Miller, Internship Site Sponsor

The United States Department of Labor

Wage and Hour Division (WHD)

(April 2010) (PDF)

Fact Sheet #71: Internship Programs Under The Fair Labor Standards Act

This fact sheet provides general information to help determine whether interns must be paid the minimum wage and overtime under the Fair Labor Standards Act for the services that they provide to "for-profit" private sector employers.

Background

The Fair Labor Standards Act (FLSA) defines the term "employ" very broadly as including to "suffer or permit to work." Covered and non-exempt individuals who are "suffered or permitted" to work must be compensated under the law for the services they perform for an employer. Internships in the "for-profit" private sector will most often be viewed as employment, unless the test described below relating to trainees is met. Interns in the "for-profit" private sector who qualify as employees rather than trainees typically must be paid at least the minimum wage and overtime compensation for hours worked over forty in a workweek. *

The Test For Unpaid Interns

There are some circumstances under which individuals who participate in "for-profit" private sector internships or training programs may do so without compensation. The Supreme Court has held that the term "suffer or permit to work" cannot be interpreted so as to make a person whose work serves only his or her own interest an employee of another who provides aid or instruction. This may apply to interns who receive training for their own educational benefit if the training meets certain criteria. The determination of whether an internship or training program meets this exclusion depends upon all of the facts and circumstances of each such program.

The following six criteria must be applied when making this determination:

1. The internship, even though it includes actual operation of the facilities of the employer, is similar to training which would be given in an educational environment;

2. The internship experience is for the benefit of the intern;

3. The intern does not displace regular employees, but works under close supervision of existing staff;

4. The employer that provides the training derives no immediate advantage from the activities of the intern; and on occasion its operations may actually be impeded;

5. The intern is not necessarily entitled to a job at the conclusion of the internship; and

6. The employer and the intern understand that the intern is not entitled to wages for the time spent in the internship.

If all of the factors listed above are met, an employment relationship does not exist under the FLSA, and the Act's minimum wage and overtime provisions do not apply to the intern. This exclusion from the definition of employment is necessarily quite narrow because the FLSA's definition of "employ" is very broad. Some of the most commonly discussed factors for "for-profit" private sector internship programs are considered below.

Similar To An Education Environment And The Primary Beneficiary Of The Activity
In general, the more an internship program is structured around a classroom or academic experience as opposed to the employer's actual operations, the more likely the internship will be viewed as an extension of the individual's educational experience (this often occurs where a college or university exercises oversight over the internship program and provides educational credit). The more the internship provides the individual with skills that can be used in multiple employment settings, as opposed to skills particular to one employer's operation, the more likely the intern would be viewed as receiving training. Under these circumstances the intern does not perform the routine work of the business on a regular and recurring basis, and the business is not dependent upon the work of the intern. On the other hand, if the interns are engaged in the operations of the employer or are performing productive work (for example, filing, performing other clerical work, or assisting customers), then the fact that they may be receiving some benefits in the form of a new skill or improved work habits will not exclude them from the FLSA's minimum wage and overtime requirements because the employer benefits from the interns' work.

Displacement And Supervision Issues
If an employer uses interns as substitutes for regular workers or to augment its existing workforce during specific time periods, these interns should be paid at least the minimum wage and overtime compensation for hours worked over forty in a workweek. If the employer would have hired additional employees or required existing staff to work additional hours had the interns not performed the work, then the interns will be viewed as employees and entitled compensation under the FLSA. Conversely, if the employer is providing job shadowing opportunities that allow an intern to learn certain functions under the close and constant supervision of regular employees, but the intern performs no or minimal work, the activity is more likely to be viewed as a bona fide education experience. On the other hand, if the intern receives the same level of supervision as the employer's regular workforce, this would suggest an employment relationship, rather than training.

Job Entitlement
The internship should be of a fixed duration, established prior to the outset of the internship. Further, unpaid internships generally should not be used by the employer as a trial period for individuals seeking employment at the conclusion of the internship period. If an intern is placed with the employer for a trial period with the expectation that he or she will then be hired on a permanent basis, that individual generally would be considered an employee under the FLSA.

Where to Obtain Additional Information
This publication is for general information and is not to be considered in the same light as official statements of position contained in the regulations.
For additional information, visit our Wage and Hour Division Website: http://www.wagehour.dol.gov and/or call our toll-free information and helpline, available 8 a.m. to 5 p.m. in your time zone, 1-866-4USWAGE (1-866-487-9243).

The FLSA makes a special exception under certain circumstances for individuals who volunteer to perform services for a state or local government agency and for individuals who volunteer for humanitarian purposes for private non-profit food banks. WHD also recognizes an exception for individuals who volunteer their time, freely and without anticipation of compensation for religious, charitable, civic, or humanitarian purposes to non-profit organizations. Unpaid internships in the public sector and for non-profit charitable organizations, where the intern volunteers without expectation of compensation, are generally permissible. WHD is reviewing the need for additional guidance on internships in the public and non-profit sectors.

U.S. Department of Labor, Frances Perkins Building, 200 Constitution Ave NW, Washington DC 20210
Telephone: 1-866-4-USA-DOL (1-866-487-2365)
http://www.dol.gov/whd/regs/compliance/whdfs71.htm

Glossary

Twenty-first-century skills

The skills such as critical thinking, problem solving, creativity, communication, team working that are needed for success in today's economy.

Apprenticeship

A period of technical training and instruction in a particular occupation, trade, art, business, or field in which the student being trained is required by legal agreement to work for an employer for a specific period of time.

Authentic assessment

A type of assessment requiring students to demonstrate skills and competencies that realistically represent tasks, problems, applications, and situations they are likely to encounter in daily life and the real world.

Behavioral-based interviews

An interview where a candidate is asked to show evidence of required competencies or behaviors.

Capstone experience

A culminating project (also known as a senior project, graduation project, or exit project) that challenges high school seniors to demonstrate their academic knowledge in an experiential way.

Coach

An adult who helps the intern to develop new skills through giving feedback and positive reinforcement.

Community assessment form

A form that helps to organize the types of possible internship sites a community may have available.

Competencies

Organizational-defined behaviors describing the behaviors required for success.

Coop   Short for cooperative education; a relative, long-duration, full-time, paid work experience in which students earn academic credit.

ELL (English Language   Students who do not speak English as their first language.
Learners)

Evidence-based   An interview in which a candidate is asked to show evidence of required competencies or behaviors.
interview

Experiential education   An approach to applied learning in which students become actively engaged in the learning process through direct experiences.

Experiential learning   Active and applied learning that directly engages and involves students in their own education.

Feedback   Objective information, both positive and constructive, about performance.

For-profit   An organization that is in business to make a profit for its shareholders.

Grunt work   Routine tasks, often undertaken by interns, that the organizations needs done on a daily basis.

Individualized learning   Instruction, training, or other educational activities implemented on a one-on-one basis with students.

Intern   Also internee; a student who is being supervised during practical training at a work site and is under the protective umbrella of the school.

Internship   A supervised learning experience in which students apply their prior knowledge to develop new skills in the real world.

Internship coordinator   The teacher or person who leads the implementation of an internship program.

Internship development   A form that helps to organize the learning opportunities available at an internship site.
form

Internship Learning   The individual learning plan that describes a series of learning goals and the activities required to meet those goals for each internship site.
Plan

Internship Quest	A company providing an online collection of materials that support internship programs with a collection of Internship Learning Plans, seminar lesson plans, and student and sponsor handbooks (www.internshipquest.com).
Job shadowing	Work-based learning experience in which a student follows or shadows an employee for a day to observe and ask questions about a particular job, position, profession or career.
Mentor	An adult who provides guidance, positive regard, and acceptance to the intern.
Not-for-profit	An incorporated organization that exists for educational or charitable reasons and from which its shareholders or trustees do not benefit financially.
Performance-based assessment	Evaluation of a student's educational progress that requires the direct demonstration of knowledge and skills. Also referred to as authentic assessment.
Portfolio assessment	A collection of student work in an internship used to document learning based on work-site work and experiences so as to receive academic credit.
Reflection	The process of putting facts, ideas, and experiences together to add new meaning to them all.
Seminars	Weekly or biweekly meetings facilitated by the teacher where interns can reflect on their experience.
Senior project	A project that challenges high school seniors to demonstrate their academic knowledge in an experiential way.
Senior slump	The last semester of high school before graduation, when seniors have completed their requirements and are no longer focused on school.
Service learning	A hands-on educational approach that combines service to the community with the classroom curriculum.
Special education	An educational alternative that focuses on teaching students with academic, behavioral, health, or physical needs that cannot sufficiently be met using traditional educational programs or techniques.

Sponsor	The individuals who represent the organization partnering with the school to offer an internship.
Sponsor handbook	A handbook for sponsors that gives specific information about the internship program.
STEM	Science, technology, engineering, and mathematics.
Student exhibition	A public showing of works or products to evaluate and assess achievement and successful completion of an internship learning experience.
Student handbook	A handbook for students that welcomes them as interns and gives detailed information for the completion of their Internship Learning Plan.
Student journal	The private writing of students reflecting on their internship which is completed during their placement.
Student orientation	Information or items a student needs to know before starting an internship.
Student presentation	A presentation by the student showing work or product for assessment.
Supervisor	The workplace adult who supervises the day-to-day activities of the intern.
TED	TED is a non-profit devoted to "Ideas Worth Spreading." It started out (in 1984) as a conference bringing together people from three worlds: technology, entertainment, design. Its talks, blogs, and conversations can be found at www.ted.com.
Uniform goals	Goals for the internship site that are common across all career areas.
Work-based learning	Opportunities to explore careers in such school-to-work programs as job shadowing, internships, and full apprenticeships.

Works Consulted

Adams, Caralee J. "Internships Help Students Prepare for Workplace." *Education Week*, January 30, 2013. www.edweek.org/ew/articles/2013/01/30/19internship_ep.h32.html?tkn=RRZ FP0oFcFfP12gPvr+6KdgwXa6W4oXc5RPD.

———. "'Soft Skills' Pushed as Part of College Readiness." *Education Week*, November 13, 2012. Accessed January 12, 2013. www.edweek.org/ew/articles/2012/11/14/12softskil ls_ep.h32.html?tkn=UOBFRWrqBIk8THG6XmVUMZKNZiFk6Oa4abdn.

Association for Career and Technical Education. *Career and Technical Education's Role in Dropout Prevention*. ACTE Issue Brief. June 2007. www.acteonline.org/issuebriefs/# .UdbUchYzhbw.

Association for Supervision and Curriculum Development. "The ASCD High School Reform Proposal." *ASCD News and Issues: The Legislative Agenda*. 2006. www.ascd.org/ASCD/ pdf/newsandissues/High%20School%20Reform%20One%20Page%20Summary.pdf.

Auguste, Byron, Susan Lund, James Manyika, and Sreenivas Ramaswamy. *Help Wanted: The Future of Work in Advanced Economies.* Report. March 2012. Accessed January 12, 2013. www.mckinsey.com/insights/mgi/research/labor_markets/future_of_work_in_advanced_ economies.

Bailey, Thomas R., Katherine L. Hughes, and David Thornton Moore. *Working Knowledge: Work-Based Learning and Education Reform*. New York: Routledge, 2004.

Berman, Sally. *Service Learning: A Guide to Planning, Implementing, and Assessing Student Projects*. Thousand Oaks, CA: Corwin Press, 2006.

Bottoms, Gene, Alice Presson, and Mary Johnson. *Making High Schools Work: Through Integration of Academic and Vocational Education*. Atlanta, GA: Southern Regional Education Board, 1992.

Bridgeland, John M., John J. DiIulio, Jr., and Karen B. Morison. *The Silent Epidemic: Perspectives of High School Dropouts.* Report. March 2006. http://docs.gatesfoundation.org/united-states/documents/thesilentepidemic3-06final.pdf.

Career Builder. "More Employers Finding Reasons Not to Hire Candidates on Social Media, Finds CareerBuilder Survey." *Career Builder: Press Room* (web log), June 27, 2013. www .careerbuilder.com/share/aboutus/pressreleasesdetail.aspx?sd=6%2F26%2F2013&id=pr766 &ed=12%2F31%2F2013.

Carnavele, Anthony P., Nicole Smith, and Jeff Strohl. *Help Wanted: Projections of Jobs and Education Requirements through 2018*. Report. Washington, DC: Center on Education and the Workforce, Georgetown University, 2010. www9.georgetown.edu/grad/gppi/hpi/cew/pdfs/FullReport.pdf.

Collins, Pauline. "The Interpersonal Vicissitudes of Mentorship: An Exploratory Study of the Field Supervisor-Student Relationship." *Clinical Supervisor* 11, no. 1 (1993): 121–35.

Common Core State Standards Initiative. Accessed December 15, 2012. www.corestandards.org.

Conference Board, The Corporate Voices for Working Families, Partnership for 21st Century Skills, and Society for Human Resource Management. *Are They Really Ready to Work? Employers' Perspectives on the Basic Knowledge and Applied Skills of New Entrants to the 21st Century U.S. Workforce Contents.* Report. Accessed January 11, 2013. www.p21.org/storage/documents/FINAL_REPORT_PDF09-29-06.pdf.

Conrad, Dan, and Diane Hedin. *National Assessment of Experiential Education: A Final Report.* Report no. ED223765. St. Paul, MN: Center for Youth Development and Research, 1981.

Dewey, John. *How We Think: A Restatement of the Relation of Reflective Thinking to the Educative Process.* Boston, MA: D.C. Heath, 1933.

———. *Experience and Education.* New York: Macmillan, 1938.

Diakiw, Jerry Y. "It's Time for a New Kind of High School." *Education Week*, May 8, 2012, commentary. Accessed July 5, 2013. www.edweek.org/ew/articles/2012/05/09/30diakiw.h31.html?tkn=PUZFAY9pb4nUW4mry7d26ByeUuj7h3nRC66e.

Diambra, Joel F., Kylie G. Cole-Zakrzewski, and Josh Booher. "A Comparison of Internship Stage Models: Evidence from Intern Experiences." *Journal of Experiential Education* 27, no. 2 (2004): 192–212.

DiMartino, Joseph, and John H. Clarke. *Personalizing the High School Experience for Each Student.* Alexandria, VA: Association for Supervision and Curriculum Development, 2008.

Edutopia. "Real-World Internships Lead to College and Career Readiness. Featuring MC2 STEM High School, Cleveland, Ohio." Edutopia video, 6:38. February 27, 2013. www.edutopia.org/stw-college-career-stem-video.

Friedman, Thomas L. *The World Is Flat: A Brief History of the Twenty-First Century.* New York: Farrar, Straus & Giroux, 2005.

Glading, Randall G. *Overcoming the Senior Slump: Meeting the Challenge with Internships.* Lanham, MD: Rowman & Littlefield Education, 2008.

Gramlich, Meredith, Kelli Crane, Kris Peterson, and Pam Stenhem. *Work-Based Learning and Future Employment for Youth: A Guide for Parents and Guardians.* Report. National Center on Secondary Education and Transition. October 2003. Accessed July 5, 2013. www.ncset.org/publications/viewdesc.asp?id=1222.

Griffin, Ricky W., and Gregory Moorhead. *Organizational Behavior: Managing People and Organizations.* 4th ed. New York: Houghton Mifflin, 2007.

Gross, Lynne S. *The Internship Experience.* Belmont, CA: Wadsworth, 1981.

Harvard Graduate School of Education. *Pathways to Prosperity: Meeting the Challenge of Preparing Young Americans for the 21st Century.* Report. Harvard Graduate School of Education. February 2011. www.gse.harvard.edu/news_events/features/2011/Pathways_to_Prosperity_Feb2011.pdf.

Harwell, Sandra H. *Career and Technical Education for College and Career Readiness: Convergence of Academics and CTE.* Rexford, NY: International Center for Leadership in Education, 2012.

Hazelhurst, David. "Chapter 15: Designing Stories." In *Changing the Fourth Estate: Essays on South African Journalism*, edited by Adrian Hadland, 154. Cape Town, South Africa: HSRC, 2005.

Herring, Sam. *Transforming the Workplace: Critical Skills and Learning Methods for the Successful 21st Century Worker*. March 22, 2012. Accessed January 11, 2013. http://bigthink.com/experts-corner/transforming-the-workplace-critical-skills-and-learning-methods-for-the-successful-21st-century-worker.

Hess, Patricia F. *Seminar Support Manual*. Centerville, MA: Internship Quest LLC, 2007.

Hess, Patricia F., and Joan E. McLachlan. *Building 21st Century Skills through Internships and Service Learning*. Centerville, MA: Internship Quest LLC, 2008.

———. *Evaluating Internships and Service Learning: Using Performance-Based Assessment to Measure Success*. Centerville, MA: Internship Quest LLC, 2008.

———. *Student Orientation Guide for Internships and Service Learning*. Centerville, MA: Internship Quest LLC, 2008.

Inkster, Robert P., and Roseanna Gaye Ross. *The Internship as Partnership: A Handbook for Campus-Based Coordinators and Advisors*. Raleigh, NC: National Society for Experiential Education, 1995.

Katz, Joan. *Evaluation of the 1992/93 City-as-School Replication Project (OREA Report)*. ERIC document reproduction service no. ED373136. Brooklyn, NY: Office of Research, Evaluation, and Assessment, NYC Board of Education, 1993.

Kiser, Pamela Myers. *The Human Services Internship: Getting the Most from Your Experience*. 3rd ed. Independence, KY: Brooks/Cole, Cengage Learning, 2012.

Klein, Alyson. Comment on *Obama Urges Big Preschool Expansion in State of the Union Speech*. February 12, 2013. http://blogs.edweek.org/edweek/campaign-k-12/2013/02/obama_urges_big_preschool_expa.html.

Kolb, David A. *Experiential Learning: Experience as the Source of Learning and Development*. Englewood Cliffs, NJ: Prentice Hall, 1984.

Levine, Eliot. "The Rigors and Rewards of Internships." *Educational Leadership* 68, no. 1 (September 2010): 44–48.

Littky, Dennis, and Samantha Grabelle. *The Big Picture: Education Is Everyone's Business*. Alexandria, VA: Association for Supervision and Curriculum Development, 2004.

McLachlan, Joan E., and Patricia F. Hess. *Building a Quality Internship/Service Learning Program*. Centerville, MA: Internship Quest LLC, 2008.

———. *A Guide to Internship Program Development and Management*. Centerville, MA: Internship Quest LLC, 2007.

———. *Internship Learning Plans*. Centerville, MA: Internship Quest LLC, 2007.

———. "Internships: An Avenue to Graduation for Today's At-Risk Students." *Silhouettes: Journal of NAREN (National At-Risk Education Network)*, winter 2008. www.atriskeducation.net; www.internshipquest.com/pdf/naren_article.pdf.

———. *Monitoring Students in Internships and Service Learning*. Centerville, MA: Internship Quest LLC, 2008.

———. *Predictable Internship Stages: Helping Your Students Succeed in Internships and Service Learning*. Centerville, MA: Internship Quest LLC, 2008.

———. *Sponsor Handbook*. Centerville, MA: Internship Quest LLC, 2007.

———. *Student Handbook: Internship Handbook and Portfolio*. Centerville, MA: Internship Quest LLC, 2007.

Merrit, R. D. *Student Internships*. Student Internships: Research Starters Education 1. Research Starters—Education, EBSCOHost. June 2008. Accessed July 9, 2013. http://www.ebscchost.com/uploads/imported/thisTopic-dbTopic-1072.pdf.

Milliken, Bill. *The Last Dropout: Stop the Epidemic!* Carlsbad, CA: Hay House, 2007.

National Academy Foundation. *Preparing Youth for Life: The Gold Standards for High School Internships*. Report. New York: National Academy Foundation, 2012.

National Association of State Directors. *The 16 Career Clusters®*. National Association of State Directors of Career Technical Education Consortium. Accessed May 15, 2013. www.careertech.org/career-clusters/glance/clusters-occupations.html.

National High School Center. *College and Career Development Organizer*. National High School Center at the American Institutes of Research. March 2012. Accessed January 11, 2013. www.betterhighschools.org/documents/NHSC_CCROrganizerMar2012.pdf.

Olson, Lynn. *The School-to-Work Revolution: How Employers and Educators Are Joining Forces to Prepare Tomorrow's Skilled Workforce*. Reading, MA: Addison-Wesley, 1997.

Palmer, Kimberly. "7 Things Employers Want from New Grads." *US News and World Report: Money: Alpha Consumer* (web log), May 15, 2012. http://money.usnews.com/money/blogs/alpha-consumer/2012/05/15/7-things-employers-want-from -new-grads.

Peacock, Louisa. "Britain's Young People Have the Wrong Skills for the Workplace, Warn Business Leaders." *The Telegraph*, March 28, 2011. Accessed January 12, 2013. http://www.telegraph.co.uk/finance/jobs/8409795/Britains-young-people-have-the-wrong-skills-for-workplace-warn-business-leaders.html.

Pete, Brian. "Unstoppable." *The Partnership for 21st Century Skills | Tools and Resources | P21 Blog* (web log), June 2012. www.p21.org/tools-and-resources/p21blog?start=21.

Peters, Tom. *Leadership*. Essentials series (DK Publishing). New York: DK Publishing, 2005.

Pierson, Rita. "Every Kid Needs a Champion." TED Talks: Education, 7:48. May 2013. Accessed July 2, 2013. www.ted.com/talks/rita_pierson_every_kid_needs_a_champion.

Robinson, Kenneth. "How to Escape Education's Death Valley." TED Talks: Education, 19:11. May 2013. www.ted.com/talks/ken_robinson_how_to_escape_education_s_death_valley.html.

Silverman, Jerry, and Margaret L. Deland. "Developing an Internship Program That Benefits Everyone." *Lab Animal* 33, no. 2 (February 2004): 34–38. www.ncbi.nlm.nih.gov/pubmed/15235644.

Society for Human Resource Management. *Critical Skills, Needs and Resources for the Changing Workforce*. Report. June 2008. Accessed January 12, 2013. www.shrm.org/research/surveyfindings/articles/documents/critical%20skills%20needs%20and%20resources%20for%20the%20changing%20workforce%20survey%20report.pdf.

Spradlin, J. Isaac. *The Evolution of Interns: Forbes*. April 27, 2009. Accessed July 1, 2013. www.forbes.com/2009/04/27/intern-history-apprenticeship-leadership-careers-jobs.html.

Steinberg, Adria. *Real Learning, Real Work: School-to-Work as High School Reform*. New York: Routledge, 1998.

Sweitzer, H. Frederick., and Mary A. King. *The Successful Internship: Personal, Professional, and Civic Development*. Belmont, CA: Brooks/Cole, 2009.

Tyson, Laura. *Closing America's Jobs Deficit*. October 15, 2012. Accessed January 12, 2013. www.project-syndicate.org/commentary/schools--skills--and-jobs-in-the-united-states-by-laura-tyson.

U.S. Department of Labor. Wage and Hour Division. *Fact Sheet #71: Internship Programs under the Fair Labor Standards Act*. 2010. www.dol.gov/whd/regs/compliance/whdfs71.pdf.

Wagner, Tony. *The Global Achievement Gap: Why Even Our Best Schools Don't Teach the New Survival Skills Our Children Need—and What We Can Do about It*. New York: Basic Books, 2008.

———. "Play, Passion, Purpose. Independently Organized TED Event." TEDxNYED, 14:50. April 28, 2012. www.tedxtalks.ted.com/search/?=Tony+Wagner.

Wiseman, Paul. "Firms Seek Grads Who Can Think Fast, Work in Teams." *Bloomberg Business Week: News*, June 24, 2013. www.businessweek.com/ap/2013-06-24/firms-seek-grads-who-can-think-fast-work-in-teams.

Index

academic skills, 70
academic standards, xx
accidents and injuries, 3–4, 23
accomplishment, 91–94
administrative issues: child-labor laws, 4; credit granting, 4; funding, 4; liability, 3; scheduling, 5; transportation, 4
Ali, Muhammad, 37
alternative education, 98–103
anticipation, 86–87
apprenticeships, xviii, 53
assessment, xxiii; Authentic Assessment, xxiii; Community Assessment Form, 18, *19*; final, 73–77; individual, 77, 82; ongoing, 70–73; online, 83; performance-based, xxiii, 50, 70, 73; standards, 78; student, 76–78. *See also* evaluation
at-risk youth, 98–103
Authentic Assessment, xxiii

Bailey, Thomas R., 1, 51
behavioral competencies, 59, 62, 64
brainstorming, 18
budgets, xxiii, 106

capstone experience, 10
career and technical education programs (CTEs), 100–101
career clusters, 34, *35–36*, 37, 106; internship coordinator and, 38
careers: awareness, 76; career-path research, 71; visible, 33

Center on Education and the Workforce, xix, xxvin3
champions, xxiv–xxv
charter schools, 103
child-labor laws, 4
coaches: coaching guidelines, 66; interns, xxi; as mentors, xxiii, 52, 65–67; reflection and, 65–67; skills, 66; supervisors, 66–67
collaboration, xx, 26
communication, 62, *63*; written and oral, xx
Community Assessment Form, 18, *19*
community needs, 12, *15*
competencies, xx, 26; behavioral, 59, 62, 64; defined, 59; doubting, 88; workplace, 62
conflict, 57–58
continuation high schools, 99
cooperative education, 101
credit granting, 4
credit recovery, 98–103
critical thinking, xviii, xx, 59, 61, 73–74. *See also* problem-solving
CTEs. *See* career and technical education programs
culmination, 94–95
curriculum, xxii, xxiv; publishing, xxv; specific to site, 11; students' needs, 9

Dewey, John, 17, 59
Diambra, Joel F., 85
District Liability Statement, 22
dropout prevention and retrieval, 98–103

early college high schools, 103
education: alternative, 98–103; Center
    on Education and the Workforce,
    xix, xxvin3; cooperative, 101; CTEs,
    100–101; experiential, 102; National
    Association of State Directors of
    Career Technical Education, 34; special
    education, xxi, 32, 99; standards, 21, 24
English Language Learner (ELL), 32, 99
evaluation: feedback role, 69–70; final
    assessment, 73–77; Internship Learning
    Plan, 28–29, 50; measurement rubrics,
    77–82, *78–83*; methods, 28–29; ongoing
    assessment, 70–73; online assessment,
    83; performance-based assessment, 70;
    sponsor, 78–79; student, 5, 78–79, 82;
    student self-evaluation, 28; students'
    needs, 10
evidence-based interviews, 77
expectations, 11, 87–89
experiential education, 102
experiential learning, 99, 101
extended-day programs, 103

face-to-face seminars, 66–67
facing issues, 89–91
Fair Labor Standards Act, 4
feedback, xvii, xx, xxii; gathering, xxv;
    internship site visit providing, 47;
    positive, 105; role in evaluation, 69–70;
    students' needs, 10
field visits, 46, 49
final assessment: individual assessment,
    77; sponsor evaluation, 78; student
    exhibition, 76; student portfolio, 73–74;
    student presentation, 75–76; student self-
    evaluation, 77–78
for profit, xviii–xix, 37, 62, 74, 76
funding, 4, 106

grants, 106
group visits, 3
grunt work, 46, 49

hands-on experience, 54, 72, 101
home schools, 103
"How to Escape Education's Death Valley,"
    98

*The Human Services Internship: Getting the
    Most from Your Experience* (Kiser), 86

independence, 91–94
independent study programs, 103
individual assessment, 77, 82
individual goals and activities, 70–73
individual learning, 95, 100
Inkster, Robert P., 45
interns: access to internship coordinator, 47;
    in adult world, 64; coach, xix; on first
    day, 55; grunt work, 46, 49; knowledge
    needed, 55; needs, 32, 55, 57; sponsor
    knowledge before arrival, 52–55;
    sponsor's five-step learning outline, 54.
    See also student orientation; students'
    needs
internship coordinator, 9, 10–11; access to,
    47; career clusters and, 38; as liaison,
    33, 50; questions for, 20; warning signs
    of problems, 49. *See also* monitoring
    students
Internship Development Form, 22
Internship Learning Plan, 19–20, 22–29,
    72, 106; development, 25–29; essential
    information, 25–26; evaluation, 28–29,
    50; organization, 29; uniform goals,
    26–28, *27*; writing, 24
Internship Quest, 106
internships: budgets, xxiii, 106; building
    sustainable, xxiii–xxiv; challenges,
    105; coordinator, 9–11; defined, xviii;
    focus, xviii; goals, xx; grants and, 106;
    implementing, 106; paid and unpaid,
    xviii, 3, 52; placement, xviii; power of,
    97–103; school's definition, 52; set-up,
    1; for sponsoring organizations, xxv;
    sponsor preparation, 52–57; for students,
    xx; supervisors, 20, 69; tips for starting,
    xxiv–xxv. *See also* quality internships;
    specific topics
internships, key elements, *7–8*;
    administrative issues, 3–5; community
    needs, 12, *15*; forms, 5–6; overview, 1–2;
    parents' needs, 12; personnel, 5; schools'
    needs, 10–11, *14*; sponsors' needs,
    11–12, *15*; students' needs, 6–10, *13–14*;
    support, 2; technology and office support,

5; timeline, 2; vision and plan, 2; write everything down, 2

Internship Site Development Form, *22*

internship site visit: components, 48; Internship Learning Plan writing, 24; in monitoring students, 47–49; providing feedback, 47; purpose, 47; school expectations, 23–24; sponsor expectations, 24; structure, 48–49; unsuitable sites, 24; what to cover, 23; what to take, 21–22

internship stages: accomplishment and independence, 91–94; anticipation, 86–87; culmination, 94–95; expectations vs. reality, 87–89; facing issues, 89–91; overview, 85–86

The Internship as Partnership: A Handbook For Campus-Based Coordinators and Advisors (Inkster, Ross), 86

interviews, 17; documents needed, 39; evidence-based, 77; setting up, 32–33; sponsor, 21, 23, 27, 31, 38–39; as stretch, 25; student, 38–39

job shadowing, xviii, 3

journals, 60; ongoing assessment and, 71; for reflection, 61; reviewing, 48

King, Mary A., 86

Kiser, Pamela Myers, 86

language: ELL, 32, 99; skills, 32

learning: experiential, 99, 101; individual, 95, 100; reflective, 61–65; service, xxi, 102; SLCs, 103; sponsor's five-step learning outline, 54; standards, 70; work-based, xviii–xix, 32, 52, 103. *See also* Internship Learning Plan

letter of introduction, 39

Levine, Eliot, 69

liability, 3

measurement rubrics, *78–83*

mentors, 10; as coaches, xxiii, 51, 65–67; need for, 57; seminar attendance, 42; sponsor relationship, 51, 53

middle college high schools, 103

monitoring students: building relationships, 45–46; guidelines, 47–49; Internship

Learning Plan evaluation, 50; internship site visits, 47–49; role of relationships, 46–47; warning signs of problems, 49

motivation, xx, 24, 61–62, 66

National Association of State Directors of Career Technical Education, 34

new economy, ix; skills for, xix, 105

night high schools, 103

not-for-profit, xix, 37, 62

ongoing assessment: career-path research, 71; common goals and activities, 70–72; individual goals and activities, 70–73; journals and, 71; thank-you letter, 71–72

online assessment, 83

online seminars, 65–66

oral communication, xx

paid internships, xviii, 3

parents' needs, 12

performance-based assessment, xxiii, 50, 70, 73

personal awareness, xx, 62, *63*

personnel, 5

Peters, Tom, 31

Pierson, Rita, 46

placement, xviii, 6–9; building choice, 34; career clusters, 34, *35–36*, 37; dreaming big, 37–38; internships for all, 31–32; overview, 31; process, 32–38; student and sponsor interviews, 38–39; student orientation, 40–42; tracking internship sites, 38

portfolio assessment, 70. *See also* student portfolio

problem solving, xviii, 60, 75, 90

public relations, xxiv, 12; building, xxv; plan for, 6

quality internships, xvii, xxv, 1; checklist, *13–15*; developing, 105; elements, 102; key elements, 6–13

quality standards, 62

real-world skills, xviii–xix, 62, 73, 86, 95

referrals, 18

reflection, 59; coaching and, 65–67; framework for reflective learning, 61–65;

journals for, 61; practice and, xxii; role
    of, 60–67; self-efficacy and, 65
résumés, 27, 39, 64–65, 71
Robinson, Ken, 98
Ross, Roseanna Gaye, 45, 86
Rotary, 18

safe environment, 64, 94
scheduling, 5, 46, 48, 103, 106
schools: charter schools, 103; continuation
    high schools, 100; culture, xxv; early
    college high schools, 103; expectations,
    23–24; home schools, 103; internship
    defined, 52; middle college high schools,
    103; needs, 10–11, *14*; night high schools,
    103; summer schools, 103; year-round
    schools, 103
self-efficacy, 65
seminars, 9, 11; content, 62; face-to-face,
    67; mentor attendance, 42; online, 67;
    overview, 59; process, 62–64; questions
    for, 61; role of reflection, 60–67; typical
    plan, 65
senior project, xxi, 101–2
senior slump, xxi
service learning, xxi, 102
site development: development process,
    20–24; examples of suitable and
    unsuitable, 20; finding sponsors, 17–20;
    Internship Learning Plan development,
    25–29; Internship Site Development
    Form, *22*; internship site visit, 21–24;
    overview, 17
skills: academic, 70; boring, 46; building, 11,
    64; coaching, 66; critical, 45; language,
    32; for new economy, xix, 105; problem
    solving, 61, 75; real-world, xviii–xix, 62,
    73, 86, 95; social, 6, 60; technical, 59, 74;
    21st century, xxi; unique, 85; workplace,
    70
Skype, xxii, 48
small learning communities (SLCs), 103
social skills, 6, 60
special education, xxi, 32, 99
sponsor evaluation, 78, 83
sponsor handbook, 52
sponsors, xx; finding in site development,
    17–20; on first day, 55; five-step
    learning outline for interns, 54; handling

conflict, 57–58; initial visit expectations,
    24; internship benefits, 53; internship
    preparation, 52–57; interviews and, 21,
    23, 27, 31, 38–39; knowing what interns
    want, 55, 57; knowledge before intern
    arrives, 52–55; mentor relationship, 51,
    53; needs, 11–12, *15*; private meetings,
    49; relationships, 51–52; reminders about
    young people, 53–54; standards, 23;
    student orientation checklist, 55, *56*; as
    supervisors, 49, 51–54, 57; supporting,
    51–58; what interns need to know, 55;
    what is expected of, 52–53. *See also*
    coaches; supervisors
standards, 4, 11; academic, xxiv; assessment,
    78; education, 21, 24; exacting, 47;
    learning, 70; quality, 62; robust, 73;
    sponsor, 23; for success, 70, 77
statistics, xxv
STEM academies, 103
student assessment, 77–78
student evaluation, 5, 77, 79
student exhibition, 76, 81
student handbook, 25, 28, 106
student orientation, 33; attendance policies,
    40–41; attire and grooming, 41; cell
    phone use, 41; confidentiality issues,
    42; end-of-internship evaluation, 42;
    equipment and supplies policies, 41;
    primary responsibilities, 40; schedule,
    safety, behavior, 41; seminars and
    mentoring sessions, 42; social
    networking, 42; sponsor checklist, 55, *56*;
    travel to site, 42
student portfolio, xxiii, 73–74, 78
student presentation, 75–76, 79
student self-evaluation, 77, 82
students' needs, *13–14*; capstone experience,
    10; curriculum, 9; feedback and
    evaluation, 10; mentors, 10; quality
    placements, 6–9; seminars, 9; supervision
    and direction, 9
*The Successful Internship: Personal,
    Professional, and Civic Development*
    (Sweitzer, King), 86
summer schools, 103
supervisors, xxi, xxiii, 9; assignments from,
    91; coaches, 66–67; complaints about,
    59; enabling, 6; influence, 65; internship,

20, 69; sponsors as, 49, 51–54, 57;
  workplace, 10
support, 10–11; internship key element, 2;
  office, 5; for sponsors, 51–58
Sweitzer, H. Frederick, 86

teacher burnout, 105
teamwork, xviii, 57, 61, *63*, 75
technical skills, 59, 74
technology, xvii, 5
TED Talks, xx, 46, 98
thank-you letter, 28, 71–72
timeline, 2
transportation, 4, 100
twenty-first-century skills, xix–xxi

uniform goals, *27*; career path, 26;
  description for transcript, 27–28; entry
  for résumé, 27; Internship Learning
Plan, 26–28; journal, 26; literature, 26;
  organization/business structure, 27;
  sponsor interview, 27; student self-
  evaluation, 28; thank-you letter, 28;
  vocabulary, 27
unpaid internships, xviii, 3

visible careers, 33
vision, 2

Wagner, Tony, xx
work-based learning, xviii, xxii, 32, 52, 103
work-based trips, 3
workers' compensation, 3
workplace competencies, 62
workplace skills, 70
written communication, xx

year-round schools, 103

About the Authors

Joan E. McLachlan is director of Internship Quest, LLC, an educational consulting and publishing firm specializing in career internship program development, staff training and development workshops, and seminars. She has also presented frequently at national education conferences on the subject of high school internships.

Joan's work with internships began almost thirty years ago when she served as project director and primary trainer for the USDOE National Diffusion Network City-As-School High School Replication Project in New York City.

As project director and trainer, she designed training materials, conducted replication trainings and presentations nationwide, and directed a team of trainers in replicating the validated internship/alternative school model across the country. She has also worked with the New York City Board of Education both as the project director and grant writer for the City-As-School School-to-Work and Career Pathways Pilot Projects.

Joan also works with the evaluation division of Measurement Incorporated on various educational research and evaluation projects. In addition, she has been a consultant to the Nassau County (NY) High School Principals' Association's Senior Year Network for over fifteen years.

During her thirty years in education, she has also taught library research, English as a second language, special education, writing, and English, both at the secondary level and as an adjunct at Baruch College in New York City.

Joan is a graduate of Westminster College (BA), Hunter College (MS), and Pratt Institute (MLS), and holds certification in school and school district administration, special education, English, and library media. She currently resides in Centerville, Massachusetts, on Cape Cod.

Patricia F. Hess is associate director of Internship Quest, LLC, where her focus is on the development of work-based skills and competencies. She develops seminars and learning experiences to help students learn the behaviors, soft skills, and positive work attitudes and habits needed for successful employment.

Patricia's background includes both teaching and international HR management. She is currently teaching organizational behavior at the University of Massachusetts-Dartmouth in the graduate and undergraduate programs, where she has developed online learning courses in Blackboard Vista and Blackboard Learn. She taught for ten years with the New York City Board of Education, working in alternative education programs.

She has worked for over twenty-five years in corporate management, focusing on management development, change management, succession, and talent development.

Patricia has consulted with a number of international companies in leadership development, employee education, and customer service. She also has wide experience in recruitment interviewing for frontline customer-service roles and entry-level jobs.

As a member of two UK government task forces, she has been involved in establishing employment policies to encourage single parents and disadvantaged groups back into the workforce.

Patricia currently lives in Brewster on Cape Cod and is a graduate of Adelphi University (BA and MS) and Cass Business School City University, London (MBA).